SO-ACH-252

PRO FOOTBALL '81

Stars, Photographs, and League Records

by Bear Kirow

Weekly Reader Books
Middletown, Connecticut

For Allen Case, Jr.

Publishing, Executive, and Editorial Offices:
Weekly Reader Books
Middletown, CT 06457

Lee Roy Selmon photos courtesy Tampa Bay Buccaneers
Earl Campbell photo from Wide World
All other photos by Vernon J. Biever

1 2 3 4 5 / 85 84 83 82 81

CONTENTS

I PROFILES

II RAMBLING TO PAYDIRT!

III 1980 STATISTICS

I
PROFILES

Jim Plunkett

JIM PLUNKETT. SUPER BOWL HERO. Super Bowl Most Valuable Player. That is today. Yesterday? It was Jim Plunkett, Castoff, Has-Been, Flop.

Not long ago he was standing in the noisy and happy Oakland dressing room after the Super Bowl victory, and he was being told that *Sport* magazine in its annual selection had named him MVP of the Super Bowl.

Incredible. But true.

At the beginning of the season he was a reserve quarterback on the team with little hope of playing very much.

And for ten years before that his career was rocky to virtually nonexistent. He had been ready to quit before the Raiders owner Al Davis took a chance and resurrected him.

Now he stood on the podium in the locker room, looking like anything but a dashing hero. Wet hair, bulging midsection, and heavy thighs that make his feet root whenever he attempts to move in the pocket. But, as Thom Greer of the

New York Daily News noted, "as far as the Raiders were concerned, he looked better than a newly minted silver dollar."

"I've shown a lot of people . . . but I'm more interested in what I've shown myself . . . that I can play quarterback in the NFL," he said. He didn't say this, but everyone knew it was true: Jim Plunkett has character.

An insightful point about the character of Jim Plunkett was made by *New York Times* sports columnist Dave Anderson after the Raiders victory over San Diego in the NFC championship game.

The Raiders were leading 34–27 with 1 minute 52 seconds remaining in the game. The Chargers had taken a time-out and Jim Plunkett walked over to talk with his coach, Tom Flores, about their third-and-4 situation at the Charger 29-yard line.

"How about a quarterback draw?" Jim Plunkett asked.

Flores told him no, that he wanted a pass play instead.

"But when I dropped back, I saw that they had gone back in their coverages and that I had some running room," Plunkett said later. "So I took off."

He sprinted for a 5-yard gain, a first down and a trip to Super Bowl XV against the Eagles.

"But significantly," said Anderson, "he had taken the responsibility upon himself.

"Some quarterbacks would have taken the easy way out: throw the ball, as the coach had ordered. If the play didn't work, then it was the coach's call, not his. Some quarterbacks would have settled for an incompletion and a field-goal attempt on fourth down, rather than running for the first down and perhaps fumbling."

But throughout his life, Raiders star Jim Plunkett

has never backed down from a challenge, beginning when he was born to two blind parents of Mexican, German and Irish ancestry 32 years ago. His late father owned a newsstand in San Jose, Calif. His mother had gone blind at 21, before her marriage.

Plunkett may be the only Frank Merriwell story left in football.

From a poor, disadvantaged household, he used his athletic abilities as a high school football star to gain a scholarship to Stanford University, in nearby Palo Alto.

He became an All-American quarterback, led his team to a Pacific-8 title and a victory in the Rose Bowl. He was named that season (his senior year, 1970), the Heisman Trophy winner, which stands for the best college football player in the country.

For the dark, curly-haired 6-2, 205-pound Plunkett (who, incidentally, is built more like a linebacker than a quarterback), there were still a lot of wonderful moments ahead—before the fall.

He was selected as the number one draft pick by the Boston Patriots. In fact, he was the number one selection in the entire draft. And that was in a year when the first three choices were quarterbacks—Plunkett, Archie Manning of Mississippi, and Dan Pastorini of Santa Clara. He was more highly rated in some places than Joe Namath at that stage.

"I thought my career would be getting into the NFL and going right to the top," said Plunkett. "But it didn't work out that way. It got pretty rough at times."

In his first season, though, the strong-armed Plunkett was an instant folk hero as No. 1 draft choice. And he had a strong season, starting every game, throwing 19 touchdown passes (which set an NFL rookie record) and being acclaimed NFL Rookie of the Year.

"The more he learned," people around the Patriots used to say, "the worse he got."

The team got worse, too, but the Patriots were not willing to admit that. His pass protection became porous, to say the least. By the 1976 season, the Patriots had Steve Grogan at quarterback, a new young hopeful, and Plunkett became expendable. He was traded to San Francisco, the team that he had rooted for as a youngster.

By now, though, Plunkett was becoming a retread. He had undergone five shoulder and knee operations.

With the 49ers, he helped them get off to a 6–1 start in 1976, but then the club hit a snag. Plunkett criticized himself because he wasn't hitting the open receivers. He worried about his pass protection, which wasn't all that bad, claiming it affected his concentration and made him hurry his throws. The next season, Jim Plunkett was gone.

Joe Thomas, then general manager of the 49ers, said, "One thing Jim could always do was throw the long pass, but we felt he had trouble with the short gains. In general, he didn't get the job done."

Plunkett says, "I came real close to quitting after I was let go by the 49ers." The year was 1978.

Al Davis, who runs the Oakland Raiders, was interested in Plunkett. And 15 days after his release from the 49ers, he was signed as a free agent by Davis.

Yet throughout the 1978 season Plunkett did not play a single down.

"I told Jim he had to lay out a year and learn

our system," said Davis. "Quarterbacks and coaches live in a pretty private world and it's a tough life; but I told him I still believed in him; I told him I would pay him whatever he thought was a fair salary. I told him we'll make it work, we'll make it happen."

So Plunkett sat and watched Kenny Stabler direct the Raiders at quarterback.

"I was only there in body, not in spirit," said Plunkett. "I couldn't concentrate on football at all. I was thinking, 'Do I really want to do this, or do I want to do something else?'"

In 1979 the situation improved hardly at all. He threw 15 passes and completed 7—one quarter's work for many quarterbacks. But Plunkett decided to see what would happen, hoping for his chance.

He got it, though not in the way he would have wished. Five weeks into the 1980 season, Raider starting quarterback Dan Pastorini (who had been traded to Houston for Ken Stabler in the off-season) broke the tibia bone in his right leg in a Raider loss to Kansas City.

The Raiders were lucky Plunkett was around. They had kept him because, "Every team needs a backup quarterback who's been around," as Tom Flores had said. "We didn't want to let Jim get away."

The backup quarterback secured his position by leading the Raiders to six straight wins before a loss to the Eagles. The Raiders lost only once more in regular-season play, a 19–13 defeat at the hands of the Eagles. They ended the season at 11–5. The team that was supposed to go nowhere before the season began, and which was supposed to collapse completely after their first-string quarterback was lost for the season, now was in the play-offs—led by a cast-off veteran quarterback.

And it was Plunkett who made the big plays in the three straight play-off wins (over the Oilers, the Browns and the Chargers) for the NFC title.

"That Plunkett is something," said Al Davis, after the Charger game. "He had so much enthusiasm it looked like he thought he was winning the Rose Bowl again."

"There were times," says Plunkett, "when I didn't think I could come back and play again. The toughest part was making myself believe I could play again. I doubted myself.

"So many people stuck with me and encouraged me when things were bad. My mom, close friends, and Al Davis. Al kept saying, 'Keep plugging.' "

He talks to his mom before every game, and she invariably says, "Don't get hurt."

She means physically, but often the problem for Plunkett has been a psychological hurt.

Wayne Hooper, an Oakland attorney who is Plunkett's agent, says he is convinced that the physical pounding with the Patriots "forced Jim to be intimidated in San Francisco. His mental outlook was affected.

"But like I told him over and over, 'Jim, it's the time and the place.' Now he has the best offensive unit he has been associated with in ten years."

Says Plunkett, "I don't feel the same pressures I used to. Those two years on the bench gave me time to reflect on how important, or unimportant, it was what people thought of me. It's just not earth shattering any more when things happen to me.

"I don't care whether or not I proved anything to anyone else," he adds. "I proved something to myself. I proved I can play again in the NFL. I've been very fortunate. A lot of good men play long careers and never get to the Super Bowl."

Ron Jaworski

"I DON'T THINK ANY OF us ever gave up," said Ron Jaworski, as he sat, head bowed, in front of his locker in the Louisiana Superdome. This was right after the Super Bowl game in which his Philadelphia Eagles had lost to the Oakland Raiders. "Jaws," as he is called, is the team quarterback and team leader.

"We thought we were in it until that last field goal put them ahead by 17 points. Then we knew that it would be very difficult. But until then we kept feeling that we were a second-half team and that we'd make the adjustments and pull it out some way."

Jaworski had had a rough time of it. He had been chased all game by the tremendous Oakland rushing attack. Jaws was never sacked but he had trouble seeing over people hurtling toward him. And when he could see, he had trouble finding open receivers.

The Raiders had done nothing unexpected. The Raiders played almost the same way they had in a

10–7 loss to the Eagles during the regular season, only this time they played better.

"It's a tremendous disappointment in losing, but it has been a great year for this football team," he said, "and this loss can't take that away.

"Maybe what happened will just be incentive for us when next season begins. We'll be back."

If there was one player who helped most to turn the Eagles from a losing team to a bunch of winners, it would have to be Ron Jaworski.

When Jaworski arrived on the Philadelphia scene in the spring of 1977, the Eagles were, according to Ray Didinger, a Philadelphia sportswriter, "dreary." Didinger wrote, "The players were beaten down, dispirited. For years, the Dallas Cowboys and Washington Redskins stopped off in Philadelphia only to wipe their feet on their way to the play-offs. The Eagles were characterized as losers, quitters. Fans gathered behind their bench and waved dog bones."

Jaworski had come from the Los Angeles Rams in a trade for the rights to tight end Charles Young. Although he was highly regarded for his powerful throwing arm, he never achieved the regular quarterback position—he was always competing for it against Pat Haden and James Harris and John Hadl. But the Rams were winners in all of the years he was with them, averaging 12 wins a year and earning a consistent play-off berth.

So he came to Philadelphia expecting to win and to go to the play-offs. And he immediately began jabbering about it.

"He was totally unlike any other quarterback I had ever been around," said offensive tackle Stan Walters. "I had played with Ken Anderson in Cincinnati and he was very precise, very businesslike.

I had played with Roman Gabriel and Mike Boryla in Philadelphia and both were loners. They had that quarterback mystique about them.

"But this guy came along and I did a double take. He was cocky, so loose. He was cracking jokes on the practice field, cutting up in the locker room. I thought, *Hey, can this crazy man play quarterback in the National Football League?*"

Not only can he play—reading defenses, throwing a football, leading his team—he can also win.

But it didn't happen overnight. In his first season, the Eagles won only 5 games, one more than the previous season. He threw 21 interceptions, among the league leaders in that bleak department. The fans often booed but coach Dick Vermeil stuck with Jaworski.

Vermeil had been the offensive coordinator for the Rams during part of Jaworski's stay there, and he liked what he knew of him—the way, as a taxi squad rookie, he jumped into a Ram huddle and commanded the respect of veterans.

"That's something you can't coach," Vermeil had said. "I liked his native intensity. He was a competitor. I just couldn't picture him ever being a fathead."

And so when Jaworski signed five one-year contracts for a total of $850,000 and immediately became the Eagles' number one quarterback, Vermeil said, "You're my quarterback. You're going to play on your bad days until they become your good days. It may cost us three bad games in a row but you're going to start and play, no matter what."

Not only was Jaworski a leader, he had a tremendous arm, but it was not always in control.

"Dick made me into a quarterback," said Jaworski. "I know that. Before I came here I was a run-and-gun guy. I was always swinging for the fences. I'd have a guy wide open in the flat and I'd throw into double coverage 40 yards downfield. I thought I was being aggressive. Actually, I was just being dumb.

"Dick harnessed my energy. He put me in an offense he conceived. He called the plays and he brought me along at his pace. There were times when I felt like busting loose, really airing it out, but I knew I'd only be regressing. Besides," he added, with a bright smile, "I knew Dick would get ticked off."

After that first year, Vermeil put together a film reel of all of Jaworski's interceptions and near-interceptions. During the off-season the two sat in Vermeil's office at Veterans Stadium and went through it play-by-play. "Dick would say, 'Okay, what were you trying to do here?' I'd tell him," said Jaworski, "and he'd say, 'Look at your half-back over here, all alone.'

"It was painful, sitting there, watching yourself make mistake after mistake, but I learned my lesson. The cliché about taking what the defense gives you, hey, it's the truth."

The following season, 1978, the Eagles enjoyed their first winning campaign since 1966 when they compiled an identical 9–7 record. It was good enough to get them into their first post-season play-off action since 1960 when, with the testy but talented Norm Van Brocklin at quarterback, the Eagles won the NFL championship. The Eagles in 1978, though, suffered a heartbreaking 14–13 loss to Atlanta in the NFC wild-card play-off.

But Jaworski was still improving as a quarterback. "I was learning new techniques—how to throw soft, how to throw over people (defenders). I know that it takes four or five years for any quarterback to develop in the NFL."

And 1978 marked his fifth season in pro football. "Something else about Ron," says Vermeil about the irrepressible young man (he is now 30) whom the Philadelphia sportswriters called "Jaws" and "Dial-a-Quote." "It's true, he did used to talk too much. But that's all changed. Ron has matured both as a quarterback and as a man."

In 1979 Jaworski for the third straight season increased his passing yardage (2,669), and lowered his interceptions (12), and the Eagles improved their record to 11–5, tying Dallas for first in the Eastern Division.

However, a disappointing 24–17 loss to Tampa Bay kept the Eagles out of the NFC championship game.

This season the Eagles were an even better team. And Jaworski an even better quarterback.

The 6-2, 195-pound Lackawanna, N.Y., native, who played his college football at Youngstown (Ohio) State, earned the highest statistical rating for quarterbacks in the NFC in 1980. He gained 3,529 yards in the air, threw 27 touchdown passes, and had only 12 passes intercepted.

Beyond that, Philadelphia tied Dallas for the Eastern Division title of the NFC, with identical 12–4 records. The teams met in the league title game.

The Cowboys, known as "America's team," was also a perennial play-off team, a team that had gone to the Super Bowl five times, and was seeking to make it a record six.

The Eagles were underdogs in the game.

When it was over, the Eagles had become the overdogs, whipping the Cowboys 20–7.

Said Jaworski after the game, "We haven't gotten much respect, have we? Well, that's just the way we wanted it. It was part of coach Vermeil's game plan. He had us saying all week how glad we were to have the chance to play the Cowboys, what an honor it was to play such a great team. We said it over and over, and we were just building up the Cowboys for exactly what happened."

And then in the privacy of their locker room, the Eagles would listen to how Vermeil saw them wiping out Dallas. And none listened more attentively than Ron Jaworski, whom Vermeil had made into a devout believer.

"There was a time," said Jaworski, "when all I worried about was my personal statistics. I'd sit down before the season and write out all my goals—completion percentage, touchdown passes, yardage.

"This year I couldn't care less. All I wanted to do is help the Eagles win a championship.

"I love to play football. I mean it when I say I would play for nothing. I could really see myself working all week in a factory and playing in a semi-pro league on weekends. The game itself is fun, and, hey, there's nothing like the feeling you have after a win.

"I'm a pretty simple guy. I'm not into a lot of frills. To me, there's my family (wife, Liz, two young daughters) and football, and that's about it. Nobody's ever gonna confuse me with Broadway Joe. I'm not looking to get my kicks anywhere but on the field.

"I couldn't be happier than I am right now because I know I've contributed to turning a losing situation around. Four years ago, this team was a doormat.

"Today we are a Super Bowl team. Do you know how satisfying that is?"

Kenny Stabler

"SACK THE SNAKE."

The sign was draped from a railing on the second tier of the Oakland Coliseum. It was a greeting of sorts for the former Oakland quarterback, Kenny Stabler, who was now appearing in the uniform of the enemy, the Houston Oilers. The date was Sunday, December 28, 1980, a wild-card play-off game matching the two AFC teams that had made a most remarkable trade before the season began.

Houston sent its veteran first-string quarterback Dan Pastorini to Oakland for the Raiders' first-string quarterback Kenny "The Snake" Stabler.

It was the first time that starting quarterbacks were swapped man for man.

Houston had gone to the AFC title game two years in a row and lost both times, and both times the opponent was Pittsburgh. The Oilers' quarterback was Dan Pastorini. It was felt, evidently, that they needed a quarterback to get them past that one game—and into the Super Bowl.

Ken Stabler Looking To Hand Off to Earl Campbell   23

And what better man than Kenny Stabler, who was the quarterback when Oakland beat Pittsburgh in the 1976 AFC title game, and then led the Raiders to the Super Bowl win over Minnesota, 32–14.

Oakland managing partner Al Davis and Stabler were at odds. Houston management and Dan Pastorini were at odds. So a housecleaning and welcoming party all in one was arranged by and for the two clubs.

Now, by a quirk of fate, they were meeting in this play-off game.

Pastorini, however, was on the sidelines in civilian clothes, since he had broken his leg earlier in the season (and was replaced by Jim Plunkett). Stabler was crouched behind the center in the Houston offense.

The day started well enough for Stabler, who had always been one of the Raider fans' favorites when he played in Oakland. If the fans did not exactly greet him as a returning hero, neither did they boo him.

And, while virtually all of the dozens of signs draped around the concrete stadium backed the home team, there was nothing more derogatory to Stabler than "Sack the Snake."

Coach Tom Flores of Oakland was concerned about Stabler. He knew how accurate a passer he was. Flores had been a Raider assistant for seven of the ten years (and head coach for one) that Stabler quarterbacked Oakland.

"I've seen him carve up so many teams, just work them over," said Flores before the game. "On Thursday before the 1977 Super Bowl, our offensive day, we went through a whole practice and the ball only touched the ground once, and that was on a drop. John Madden, our coach then, was standing next to me, and he said, 'What do you think, Tom?' and I said, 'Throw a blanket over him and get him out of here. This is scary.' "

But Flores' fears were soon put to rest. To make it brief, the day against Oakland did not turn out well for Stabler.

He was sacked seven times by his former teammates, and saw two of his 26 passes intercepted. Oakland walloped Houston 27–7.

After the game Stabler sat in a corner of the little auxiliary dressing room, slowly peeling off his equipment. He shook his head sadly when people asked what had happened. He hadn't taken a particularly ferocious beating. In fact, the Raiders practically wore kid gloves when they tackled him, but tackle him they did. And even when Lester Hayes and Mike Davis got him on blindside shots that could have dismantled him, they chose to leap on his back rather than stick him.

Oddly, the toughest hit Stabler took was when John Matuszak, his former roommate who was a 6–8, 280-pound defensive left end, jumped offside and bowled him over.

Stabler said, "I believe you're offside, Tooz." And Matuszak replied, "I believe you're right, pardner."

And that's the way it went for Stabler, who wanted so much to beat the team that traded him away—and in the play-offs, and in Oakland. Instead, he spent most of his time looking up at the seagulls circling around the Oakland Coliseum in the late afternoon.

"It wasn't Kenny's fault," said Coach Bum Phillips. "We had a malfunction in pass protection. He didn't have time to get his arm up, let alone find a receiver."

In the trade for quarterbacks, Phillips had come to the point where he was prepared to make a large gamble. Make no mistake, it is a gamble anytime a coach breaks up the inner circle of a team that for two straight years came within one game of the Super Bowl.

As Phillips put it: "I went 11–5 last year with Dan. If we don't go 12–4, I know I will be criticized."

The team went 11–5 again, and they didn't get to the AFC title game for the first time in three years. Phillips was more than criticized. He was fired.

The Oiler players, for the most part, were unhappy about that. Phillips is an immensely popular man with most of them. Including and particularly Stabler.

With his flowing gray hair, full around the ears, and a beard flecked with pepper, Stabler, according to writer Mickey Herskowitz, looks like a cross between Kenny Rogers, the country and western singer, and one of Robin Hood's archers. With this view of Stabler, it is interesting to note how he saw Phillips in their first audience after the trade. Said Stabler:

"Right after the trade I came back from a press conference and walked into his office. He was propped up with his cowboy boots on the desk. He had a pair of ragged old Levis and a cowboy shirt, and his hat was cocked on his head. He was spittin' tobacco juice into a Coca-Cola cup. I said right then, that's my kind of guy. He's just an unpretentious cowboy who happens to coach football."

The Oilers were delighted to have Stabler. At 34, he might have seen some of his best seasons, but he was still a great passer. In fact, he was the most accurate passer in NFL history, from a statistical standpoint. Going into the 1980 season, he had connected for 59.95% of his attempts (1,489 of 2,481).

In 1980 that high percentage rose, as his completion percentage was 64.1.

Stabler's first outing with the Oilers—a 21–7 exhibition game loss to Tampa Bay in the Houston Astrodome—was a personal success. He went 9-of-15 passing (with three "drops") and guided the Oilers to their only score on an 81-yard drive in the second period. The mood of the Oiler fans was almost euphoric. Stabler was pleased by the performance, but cautious.

"I'm no savior," he said. "Who is going to save a team that went 11–5 last year?" But he also admitted: "With Earl (Campbell) running and good receivers to throw to, I imagine we can make defenses pretty nervous."

Something else made some people nervous. And that was Stabler's life-style. He is an open, fun-loving guy, who, to use Satchel Paige's term, likes the midnight ramble.

"People have always thought my life-style would ruin me," he says. "Yeah, I like to get out and get after it. So what if I go out and stay late and enjoy myself. All the time I'm doing that, I'm being nice to people. I go into nightspots and sign autographs and shake hands and shoot the breeze. What's wrong with that?

"Everybody's system is different. Some people need six or eight hours of sleep a night. Most of the time I get two hours and I'll be just fine. Yeah, I carouse. I'm completely honest about it. I don't try to hide anything.

"One thing that was always important to me,

and it will be here (in Houston) too, is to have a good rapport with the other players. I want them to like me, and work for me, and have confidence in me. I will make 'em like me."

One night when the Oiler coaches had come together after practice, Assistant Coach Joe Bugel laughed out loud. "The Snake," he said, as if he were proposing a toast, "he's beautiful. Did you see him walking out to the practice field? He caught up with Corker (John Corker, a rookie), draped his arm around his shoulder, and started talking to him."

"And Corker," said another coach with great enthusiasm, "went out to have a heck of a practice."

The players did take to Stabler, and they enjoyed playing with him, as they did in Oakland, but it takes more than harmony to make a winning football team. It takes excellence on all fronts.

And when, for example, the pass protection breaks down, as Phillips acknowledged it did in Oakland, then there is trouble ahead.

And, as Stabler says, "football is a 'we' game.

"The trouble with all the talk about 'Stabler will get Houston past Pittsburgh,' or 'Stabler can't cut it anymore,' is stuff I resent," said Stabler.

"I resented it when Al Davis put the blame on me when Oakland quit being a play-off contender. Nuclear physics is an 'I' game. But football is a 'we' game.

"I'll take the heat if I have to, just like Davis said. I'll never change my style because of what people write or say. Heck, when you bring up the time I threw seven interceptions in a game, I'll look you in the eye and tell you that, if the game had gone three more hours, I'd have thrown 15. I'm not going to stop trying to catch up just because some-body's criticizing me."

Stabler is insistent on remaining his own man, and staying above the shifting sands of public opinion.

"If," he had said before the season started, "we go all the way, I'll own Houston. If we don't, I'll be looking for a sheep ranch someplace to get away from all the abuse. But look, how many guys ever get to face those possibilities?

"Sure, I'll take the heat. Or the Super Bowl ring."

For now, anyway, it'll be heat.

Brian Sipe

NOW, IF YOU KNOW FOOTBALL, you know there is really only one thing to do in the following situation, which occurred in last season's American Football Conference play-off game between the Cleveland Browns and the Oakland Raiders in Cleveland's Municipal Stadium:

The Browns are trailing 14–12, and they have the ball on second down on the Raiders' 13-yard line with 49 seconds to play in the game.

"We figured like everybody else that they would run the ball up the middle and then kick for a field goal," Mike Davis said. The three points for the field goal would have given the Browns the winning edge. "What they did, though," added Davis, "was baffling."

Brown quarterback Brian Sipe passed!

Cleveland couldn't resist taking one more shot at making a touchdown—and insuring that the Raiders couldn't come back and kick a winning field goal themselves.

Coach Sam Rutigliano had sent the word to

Sipe: Throw the ball to wide receiver Dave Logan in the end zone. "If nobody's open," he added, "throw it into Lake Erie."

Rutigliano reckoned that if the pass was incomplete, he could use one more down to run the ball, then send in Don Cockroft to kick a field goal that figured to be no longer than 30 yards.

Many coaches would never have considered such a strategy. They would never have put the ball into the air and risked interception. Rutigliano had great confidence in the accurate arm of Sipe, though, who statistically was the leading passer based on overall performance in the National Football League, including having the lowest rate of passes intercepted, 2.5 percent.

Not only that. Sipe had led the Browns to an incredible record of come-from-behind victories. Since Rutigliano had taken over as coach in mid-1978, the team had come from behind in 14 games in the last minutes of play. Take last season's Green Bay heart-stopper: Cleveland trailed, 21–20, with 16 seconds to go. Lining up at midfield, Sipe intended to throw to wide receiver Reggie Rucker, hoping to get into field-goal range. But as he was calling signals, the entire Packer defense crept up to the line of scrimmage; it was going to be a maxi-blitz. Calmly, Sipe glanced at Dave Logan. Logan nodded, sped into the clear, grabbed Sipe's pass at the 19 and ran it in for the winning touchdown.

"The tighter the situation," Rutigliano had said, "the better Brian gets."

Now, against Oakland, Cleveland tight end Ozzie Newsome was surprised by the call, which would have him acting primarily as a decoy. After the snap, Newsome glided to the end zone. Sipe, meanwhile, had decided that Logan was covered too well.

"Lake Erie beckoned," noted Bruce Newman of *Sports Illustrated*, "but Sipe had come too far too fast to dump it in the drink." True. And when Sipe saw Newsome's large, soft paws beyond the goal line, he cranked back and heaved. The ball fluttered against the stiff head wind of this frosty day.

Suddenly Oakland safety Mike Davis cut in front of Newsome and picked the pass out of the air. Interception! The Raiders ran out the clock, and won the game.

"We lived and died with the pass all year long," said Newsome in the glum Cleveland locker room after the game. "This time we died."

And so came to an end the saga of the "Kardiac Kids" as the Browns in 1980 were known by their fans. The Raider game simply was the one rabbit they could not pull out of their hat.

It had been a marvelous season, however, one in which the Browns made the play-offs for the first time since 1972, when they lost to Miami in the first round.

It was also a remarkable year for Sipe, the darkhaired, 6-1, 195-pounder out of La Mesa, California, and San Diego State. In his eighth season as a pro, he shattered club records with 554 passing attempts, 337 completions, 30 TD tosses, and 4,132 yards gained.

Many of those records once belonged to Otto Graham, the legendary quarterback of the Browns of the 1940's and 1950's. In 1979, Graham was voted the Browns' all-time quarterback.

"If the fans vote again in five years," said Graham, "I think Sipe will be the quarterback, not me."

Says Rutigliano: "Sipe is a leader with a tremendous capacity to operate under pressure. One of the most important ingredients a quarterback needs is a great amount of confidence in himself, and Brian has had it all along. He's a battler, a competitor."

There was a time, though, when the Cleveland Browns didn't want him at all. His passes wobbled, the team stumbled in the standings, and he was benched. He didn't seem to mind. There were broader perspectives than football in his view. A long-haired campus radical, he had come to play football only because he was, he said, "seeking some kind of life experience."

Today, that experience has taken a dramatic change. Sipe has become a superb tactician on one of the best teams in professional football.

There is no simple explanation for Sipe's transformation from mediocrity to stardom.

His passes still tend to wobble—instead of the elegant spirals thrown, say, by a Dan Fouts or Steve Grogan. But Sipe compensates with uncanny accuracy.

"He's so good," says Logan, "that he rarely throws behind you or puts you in a position where you'll be hurt."

He has been criticized for not being elusive enough when dodging blitzes. But, says Browns quarterback coach Jim Shofner, "he doesn't have to be. He's so well prepared it's as if he was conceived with the game plan in him. His strongest asset is running a football game, taking the week's work, and applying it, which a lot of quarterbacks are unable to do. He's got the intelligence to analyze situations and act accordingly."

Sipe says, "I feel I reflect the team, in that I don't

think we're exceptionally talented. Actually, we're not far above the average in raw talent. I include myself in that evaluation. We're a team that plays a little above its head most of the time. That's the kind of club I enjoy playing with. We get the most out of our talent."

As for his startling quarterback prowess, he adds, "It's really a matter of instinct and what I call the intangibles. The key intangible is knowing exactly where to throw the ball. I guess some people would write that off as pure luck. It's not."

Early in his pro career, though, he wondered if he would ever be lucky enough to get the chance to play.

When the Browns selected him in the thirteenth round of the 1972 draft, it was difficult to determine who was the least enthusiastic.

"Nobody really paid much attention to me," said Sipe.

"Brian didn't seem sure he wanted to play pro football," said Cleveland Browns owner Art Modell.

Sipe, upon leaving San Diego State, had vague notions about hitchhiking through Europe and then becoming an artist. But after leading the nation's college quarterbacks in passing in 1971, he decided that he would give the pros a try.

"I was a shot-in-the-dark as far as the Browns were concerned," said Sipe. "I came to Cleveland with great hopes, but I've had to fight every step of the way.

"In high school and college I got by on natural talent, but in the pros the talent is so equal that you must be a student of the game. I had to develop many things, the most important being study habits and concentration."

For two seasons, Sipe was a member of the less-than-glamorous "taxi squad," getting $1,000 per week to work out with the team and to sit in the stands on Sundays.

"My first year I didn't work at all," Sipe says. "In practice I couldn't take a snap without fumbling the ball. I only knew two plays anyway."

That summer, he and his high school sweetheart, Jeri Frame, were married. After the marriage he seemed to settle down, but still nothing much happened with the Browns. He remained an understudy to the Browns regular quarterback Mike Phipps.

Sipe got his first chance in 1974. "The first game I ever started was against the Chargers in my hometown of San Diego," says Sipe, "and it looked like I was going to be the hero."

With less than a minute to go, San Diego was ahead, 36–35. Sipe moved the ball into field-goal range with 24 seconds to go. "All I had to do was call a quarterback sneak to set up the field goal," he recalls. "Well, I fumbled the snap and they recovered. It was the most shocking moment I've ever had in sports."

Well, possibly the *second* most shocking, after the interception thrown in the last seconds of the Raider play-off game.

But the winning or losing of one game—or two, or three—does not throw Sipe for a substantial loss. There is more to life than that, he reasons.

Now signed to a four-year, $1 million contract, Sipe finds himself not only the top passer in the game but also Cleveland's latest heartthrob, dogged by teenage girls, and middle-aged matrons. Yet Sipe keeps his head firmly on his shoulders.

He refuses to make endorsements or personal appearances, for example. And, surprisingly, he doesn't feel particularly elated when he throws a touchdown pass.

"My rewards are far more basic," he says. "It's the chance to be totally at risk and test the primal instincts."

But Sipe has one understandable and predictable ambition. "I'm obsessed with that Super Bowl ring."

Whether he gets it or not, Sipe and the Kardiac Kids are certain to cause a lot of excitement in the pursuit.

Tony Dorsett

THERE ARE THE JOKES THAT start, there's good news and there's bad news.

For Dallas running back Tony Dorsett this past season, it was no joke.

First, the good news.

"Dorsett has come along extremely well," said Dallas coach Tom Landry. "This has been his best year."

Now the bad news. It seems that he chose to play not only the worst game of this season but possibly the worst game of his career in the National Football Conference championship game, in which Dallas lost to Philadelphia 20–7.

The wire-service photograph of Dorsett lying prone on the field, his head dejectedly bowed above his clasped hands, will be etched in the memory of many football fans. And of course the scene will be etched in the mind of Tony Dorsett himself. The photo was taken shortly after he allowed a pass from Danny White to bounce off his chest for an incompletion.

Dorsett caught three passes for 27 yards in the game, but the one he missed in the fourth quarter on third down with 3 yards to go on the Eagle 32-yard line was crucial to the Dallas hopes of a touchdown drive.

Adding insult to injury, that miscue came shortly after his key fumble.

That fumble occurred with 5 minutes 42 seconds remaining in the third quarter. Jerry Robinson, Philadelphia linebacker, recovered and returned 22 yards to the Dallas 38. Six plays later the Eagles scored their second touchdown. It turned out to be the clincher.

"I'll take a lotta blame for this loss," said Dorsett, the Cowboys' fourth-year standout. "In my opinion that fumble was the turning point of the game.

"I've never had to put the blame on myself and I don't know why I'm doing it now." When it was mentioned that other teammates had also contributed to the loss, Dorsett said, "But that fumble was a big play. I'm man enough to stand up to it."

Dorsett gained 41 yards rushing in 13 attempts in the game for a 3.2 average. His longest gain was 11 yards. For someone who can reel off 20-, 30-, and 40-yard gains, and who averaged 4.3 yards per carry during the regular season, it was a lackluster performance.

"You know how I felt when I didn't catch the ball in the fourth quarter?" he asked. "I felt like using my hands as claws, tearing up the turf, and burying myself right there and then."

Coach Landry called the loss "the toughest" of the season. It prevented Dallas from going to the Super Bowl for a record sixth time. Dorsett, who starred for the University of Pittsburgh before he was drafted by the Cowboys, has been playing football for 15 years. He started in the seventh grade. He did not say his performance in the title game was his worst ever, but he did say it was not one of his better ones.

"I've had worse days than this, but it will be with me for a while. I like to think of myself as a pressure ballplayer. But this is just one of those days I didn't come through."

For most of what seems a charmed life, Tony Dorsett has come through. In fact, there are those who say he was born for stardom. Just look at his initials: T.D. Touchdown.

When he joined the Cowboys he was the Heisman Trophy winner—emblematic of the best player in the country—and he was the star of the top-rated college team in the nation, Pitt. He had been a three-time All-America, a first-round selection who had commanded four draft choices in a trade with the Seattle Seahawks, a rookie who surely would strut into training camp as an instant starter.

Not quite.

When he arrived in training camp, he was listed as a backup to halfback Preston Pearson.

And in practice Landry was critical of his new acclaimed player. Dorsett, according to Landry, was dropping too many passes.

"I know," said Dorsett. "But I'll catch those passes in the games."

"You've got to learn to catch them in practice first," said Landry.

It took Dorsett 10 regular-season games before he passed Landry's stiff tests, and became a starting back for the Dallas Cowboys.

The Cowboys went on to win the Super Bowl that season, 1977. They have not won the Super

Bowl since; but, going into the Philadelphia title game, they were favorites to beat the Eagles, on the strength of their previous game against the Los Angeles Rams. In that victory, Dorsett, who is called, in the Dallas media guide, "the most electrifying runner in Cowboy history," he gained 160 yards, averaging 7.2 yards a carry. He got the touchdown that tied the score at 13 in the second quarter on a 13-yard run, and caught a pass for the go-ahead score in the third.

The way he scored it typifies the style of Dorsett, a combination of finesse and power. He caught White's pass at the 9-yard line and turned to his right. Johnnie Johnson, the rookie safety, came from the side and lunged. He caught nothing but the place where Tony Dorsett's hips used to be. Now Rod Perry, a cornerback, waited for Dorsett at the goal line, but Dorsett put down his head and banged into Perry, knocking him down and running over him into the end zone for the critical score.

"On that touchdown pass," said Landry later, "Dorsett just scored on his own natural ability. That took some sting out of the Rams."

Dorsett is the first NFL back to gain more than 1,000 yards in each of his first four seasons. Yet Dorsett says he thinks he could produce more if he played even more.

"I don't usually carry the ball 22 times in a game. I think that's my second highest total this season. And if I did carry the ball, I think I'd be a better runner. Any back will tell you, the more you carry the ball, the better you'll run. On other teams, they repeat plays. We hardly ever repeat plays. That makes it harder too. If you repeat plays, you get a better feel of what the defense is going to do."

Landry says, "The first few years I was concerned about Tony's size." Dorsett is 5-11, a well-muscled 183 pounds. "I wanted to make sure he didn't get hurt, but I wanted to make sure he also got his thousand yards. But now I've been using him more and more and he's responded to it."

Dorsett disagrees with Landry's theory that the fewer times one carries the ball, the less the injury risk.

"I don't believe that using a back at only 50 percent of his potential will prolong his career," said Dorsett. "One play can end your career. I feel I could carry the ball 25 times a game over a full season, but if I did get injured the first thing people would say was that I was overworked."

Against the Rams he was indeed the Cowboys' workhorse. He set a club record of 338 yards gained rushing. During the season he rushed for 1,185 yards. His four-year, regular-season total is 4,624 yards. (The NFL record for a running back's first four years is 5,316, held by Walter Payton of the Chicago Bears.) But for Dorsett, those 4,624 yards aren't enough.

Landry acknowledges that Dorsett will get more and more time in the Dallas backfield.

Some people take Dorsett's outspokenness for "arrogance." But Dorsett says the opposite is true of him, that actually he is a very unsure person, so unsure that he was afraid to leave home and go away to college.

"That's why I went to Pitt," says the native of Aliquippa, Pennsylvania, a Pittsburgh suburb. "I could have gone anywhere I wanted. I wasn't ready to leave home. I was a quiet, shy kid. I didn't want to leave Mommy and Daddy.

"So if anything went wrong, I could always go home. I spent more time at home my freshman year than at school."

Tony is the youngest of four boys in the Dorsett home. He also has two sisters.

Many mothers of superstars—the mother of Gale Sayers, for one—tell stories of how clumsy their children were when young. (Sayers, the one-time Bears star running back, was always bumping into things as a tot, says his mother.) But Tony's mother remembers that "Tony would never fall off anything." He was naturally coordinated and gifted with exceptional balance, just the assets that have helped make him one of the best runners in the NFL.

Tony's motivation for being such a dedicated and serious athlete is seeing his father come home from work every night. Tony's dad worked in a dark, loud, blasting steel mill. Tony once visited his father at work and will never forget the experience. The elder Dorsett was so covered with soot that young Tony couldn't recognize him. Tony, scared that the same fate might befall him, vowed never to work there, and to develop his natural skills.

He has been the target of "cheap shots" by opponents throughout his career. The other team often tries to put the opposing star out of commission. But Tony is strong and resilient and motivated, and if he is hit, he bounces back rather quickly.

But he has also learned to avoid unnecessary contact. Sayers, in fact, has criticized him for it to an extent. Sayers said that Dorsett is too much in a hurry to run the ball out of bounds, rather than bruise ahead for an extra yard or two.

"That's bull," says Dorsett. "I don't see how Sayers can say that I'm not tough enough and I try to run for the sideline. I'm not a punishing runner. I'm a finesse runner. And if I see I'm going to be stopped, I'm going to step out of bounds.

"But not unless I see I can't get any more yards."

With all the yards that Dorsett does get—despite the last NFC title game—it's more than obvious that he knows very well what he's doing.

Lee Roy Selmon

"FROM WORST TO FIRST." THAT was the battle cry of the Tampa Bay Buccaneer football fans before the start of the 1980 season.

After the Bucs' surprisingly fine showing in 1979—they finished the season just one step away from making the Super Bowl—hopes were understandably bright.

An expansion team, beginning in 1976, the Bucs were the shock of pro football as they registered an 11–7 record in 1979 and a convincing 24–17 win over the strong Philadelphia Eagles in the opening play-off game. This came after three losing seasons in which Tampa Bay was the joke of the league. (In fact, it had lost its first 26 games—five by shutouts.)

In the NFC title game, though, the Bucs fell flat and lost to the Rams 9–0.

Everyone knew—or expected—that the Bucs, the NFC Central Division winners, would be back in 1980 stronger than ever.

The Bucs were back all right, but hardly stronger than ever.

Lee Roy Selmon puts the clamp on Fuller of Kansas City.

"From worst to first—and now back to worst," quipped coach John McKay after the final game of the 1980 season. The Bucs won just five games, lost 10, and tied one, and ended up in a tie with Green Bay for last place in the NFC's Central Division.

The orange-clad Tampa Bay team had turned into a pumpkin after a Cinderella season.

Lee Roy Selmon was one of the few exceptions to not disappoint this season.

Selmon, a 6-3, 250-pound defensive end and the Bucs first-ever draft choice out of the University of Oklahoma in 1976, enjoyed another spectacular year, capped with his selection to the Pro Bowl team.

He was the bulwark of what was expected to be the supreme defensive unit in the NFL; it was the defense which was credited with getting the Bucs to the NFC title game in the first place.

"I hope I'm wrong, but I'm afraid we are going through what Atlanta did last year," said McKay midway through the 1980 season. "They had a very strong defense that played like wildmen and took them to the play-offs in 1978. Then the same guys didn't play defense as well last year and they didn't have a good season. All it is is attitude.

"This team seems to be still living in the past. I hope they don't think they can just turn it on like a faucet because sometimes you turn it on and nothing comes out."

Lee Roy Selmon in particular was spared the coach's criticism. And for good reason. Note, for example, *The Sporting News* report of the Bucs game against the New York Giants:

"Tampa Bay's defense provided the knockout punch as the Buccaneers whipped the New York

Giants. Defensive ends Lee Roy Selmon and Bill
Kollar did the damage with 27 seconds to play in
the first half. Kollar broke through and hit quarterback Phil Simms' arm, causing a fumble which Selmon recovered. Doug Williams followed with a
25-yard TD pass to Mike Shumann with 22
seconds to go in the half.

"After the ensuing kickoff, Selmon smacked running back Billy Taylor, resulting in another fumble,
recovered by Kollar at the Giants 17. Garo Yepremian cashed in on that with a 35-yard field goal,
giving Tampa Bay a 23–0 halftime lead."

Tampa Bay went on to win 30–13, but such a
blending of the team's talents last year was seldom
seen.

Selmon, though, continued being one of the
league's best. "When you get a chance to watch
someone like Lee Roy Selmon, what you see is an
eagle going after his prey," said teammate Ricky
Bell, the Bucs' leading running back.

Ted Albrecht, offensive tackle for the Chicago
Bears, remembers the first time he played against
the Bucs and Selmon. At the half, in which the
score was 0–0, he was sitting in a corner trying to
figure out what had happened.

"I remember the coach came over to me," he
said. "He asked how I was doing. I told him my
deepest secrets. I said I never wanted to be buried
at sea. I never wanted to get hit in the mouth with
a hockey puck, and I didn't want to go out and
play that second half against Lee Roy.

"He said I'd be fine. The first play he went all
the way around me and got Bob Avellini (Bear
quarterback). Lee Roy is normal size, but there is
nothing normal about his talent. He is so quick, so
strong. There's a move he makes when he lines up

a yard and a half outside you. You try to get back to cut off his route to the quarterback, and then he'll come inside. It's a fairly common move in the league, but you've got to see him do it to believe it. . . ."

After that game, the reporters walked into the Bear dressing room where the players were joyous after beating the Bucs. The only player who was downcast was Albrecht, who sat in a corner, dazed.

"I studied Lee Roy after that," he says now. "I've played him five times and there are ways to attack him, because there are ways to attack anybody. I don't want to give away what I know, but you minimize the damages if you don't go after him the same way twice in a row.

"The thing about Lee Roy is that he has a sense of etiquette out there. He has ethics. I've wanted to say something to him for a long time—maybe just wish him good health, but there hasn't been the chance.

"During the game he's never said a word, and the way I figured it out, he doesn't want to talk. I don't want to talk, either. It seems important not to get him upset. . . ."

Rarely has Lee Roy been as upset as when the Bucs opened their doors as a franchise and proceeded to lose their first 26 games.

"It got where we dreaded Sundays," said Dewey Selmon, Lee Roy's brother and an inside linebacker on the Bucs (Dewey was the second-round draft choice of Tampa Bay in 1976). "There was a feeling. You knew you were gonna lose. You lost the spirit for the game. The fun was gone. The team was fragmented, everybody fighting for

"Watch out, here comes Lee Roy!"

his own life. Something would go wrong, and everybody'd come back saying, 'I did mine, it wasn't me. . . .' "

Lee Roy came to dread supermarkets. "People weren't rude, but it's hard going out for milk knowing six strangers are going to tell you what went wrong in the third quarter. Then one night Dewey and I were watching Johnny Carson and he said Tampa Bay had just played Samsonite Luggage and lost. I said, 'Do you believe that?' and the next thing I knew neither of us could stop laughing."

Soon, though, McKay began to build a formidable club.

The first time anyone noticed was on Sunday, December 11, 1977. The Bucs beat the New Orleans Saints—drubbed them, in fact—33–14.

The Bucs all-time record now stood at 1–26.

The Saints felt totally disgraced. Their coach said that they should burn the game films. Quarterback Archie Manning said he didn't want to show his face in public for a year.

Some day, it had been assumed by NFL opponents, the Bucs would lick an opponent. Everyone knew that. But no one wanted to be there when it happened. As in the title of Sinclair Lewis's book, each team felt *It Can't Happen Here*. Or to us.

Selmon was perhaps the single most important reason for the victory over New Orleans. Up to that point in the season he had played superbly; he led the team with 13 sacks of the quarterback.

All afternoon he chased the Saints' harried Manning from one end of the field to the other. As the Bucs began to pile up points on the scoreboard, the Saints grew more and more frazzled. The game was a nightmare to them, but was a dream come true for Selmon and his teammates.

When the team returned to Tampa, they were met at the airport by 8,000 screaming fans. It was a triumph to be savored for a long time.

Lee Roy has been savoring football moments, though, for a long time. He played in the same backfield in high school in Eufaula, Oklahoma, with his brother Dewey where they both made All-American.

Both went to Oklahoma and made All-American and Academic All-Americans. Now they were defensive linemen. In his senior year, Lee Roy won the Outland and Lombardi awards, signifying the best lineman in college football.

Football is not the only thing in Lee Roy's life, fortunately enough. He knows he must prepare for the day when his football career is over. Currently he works in a manager trainee's position in a bank in Tampa, and then returns home to his house in a quiet section of north Tampa. He lives there with his wife and two-year-old daughter.

One day after the 1980 season, Selmon, who is from a family of nine children, was talking about his life.

"In our family," he said, "we don't measure success by dollars. Certainly not by football. I'm not special from my brothers or sisters. We all try to be the best we can be. It's like that on a team too.

"We're 11 people working together. No stars, no leaders. We all lead. Reporters ask if I'm the best this or the best that. I leave that to other people to deal with.

"I just try to be as good as Lee Roy Selmon can possibly be. There's nothing more that I can do."

Terry Bradshaw

TERRY BRADSHAW COULD HARDLY BELIEVE it. There was Don Shula, the Miami Dolphin coach, shouting obscenities at him and screaming "bush."

Shula was enraged because Bradshaw, the Pittsburgh Steeler quarterback, had thrown a pass in the final seconds of a game that had already been decided, 23–10 in favor of Pittsburgh. This took place on November 30 of last season in Pittsburgh.

Bradshaw, ever sensitive, rushed over to the opposing coach, Shula, as the gun sounded and tried to explain. "I called for a short, safe pass," he said, "because I saw the defense was coming with the blitz."

Shula, who has a quick temper and felt Bradshaw was trying to run up the score and show up his team, was having none of that. "Bush," he screamed again. "You're going to get yours!"

If there was a moment to symbolize the frustration of a strange season for Terry Bradshaw, this was it. He had just led his team to victory, and he was made to feel terrible.

He had enough bad things happen during the season, however, to make him feel bad. He didn't need the good to put him into a funk too. He had been bounced around for much of the season. He'd jammed his thumb, bruised his ribs, damaged his elbow and banged up his knee. Not to mention wounding his psyche.

It developed that he changed his throwing motion, was benched for the first time in six years and second-guessed himself for not pulling out of a couple of games voluntarily when he was injured.

The lowest point of the season came on December 4, when, with the largest regular-season, prime-time TV audience in pro football history looking on, Bradshaw and the Steelers lost to Houston 6–0. It was the Steelers first shutout in a game in which Bradshaw had started in his 11-year career. He threw three interceptions, including one in the end zone on a pass from the Oilers' 6.

The loss virtually eliminated the Steelers from the play-offs, and from the opportunity to win a third straight Super Bowl championship.

Terry Bradshaw knows what number one is all about. His Steelers won the Super Bowl in 1975, 1976, 1979, and 1980. All with Terry at quarterback. He was twice the MVP of the Super Bowl— a distinction he shares with only Bart Starr—and most recently was voted to the NFL's Team of the Decade. The Steelers, many of them stars too, twice in a row picked him as their Most Valuable Player.

And that is why the game against Houston was very disappointing for Bradshaw. Until the end he had the confidence he could bring his team back to win the game. He had done as much numerous times, most notably in three of the four Super

Bowl wins, and the 1980 game was culminated by the tremendous thunderbolt touchdown pass to John Stallworth in the fourth quarter against the Rams.

He didn't return to Pittsburgh with the team after that Oiler game in early December of 1980. Instead he retreated to his 400-acre ranch in Grand Cane, Louisiana. There, he rested and fished, and reflected for four days on what had gone haywire.

"I thought about the year and what had happened," he said. "I went over all the losses and how we lost."

Pittsburgh's six losses were as many as the Steelers incurred in the 1978 and 1979 seasons combined.

When he returned to Pittsburgh, the broad cowboy hat covering his balding head, he said he felt refreshed, determined to finish the season on a victory note.

"It's like when a pitcher has his stuff and still gets knocked out," he said. "That can happen to any athlete."

Two games remained in the season. The Steelers won the first, beating Kansas City 21–16 (with Bradshaw throwing for two touchdowns); but they lost the last, to San Diego, 26–17. What was special, though, and perhaps a harbinger of the Steelers' and Bradshaw's intensity for the 1981 season, was how the San Diego game ended. With Pittsburgh behind 21–9, and the final seconds ticking away, Bradshaw, still in the game, threw a touchdown pass to tight end Bennie Cunningham, to make the score respectable. The Steelers—and Bradshaw—even in losing, were standing tall.

Bradshaw, apparently, has changed significantly in attitude in his 11-year career.

When he first came up he could fall into deep depressions at times of adversity, and his game would be severely affected.

He had gone through benchings, through a marriage and divorce in 1974, to a rocky marriage to ice-skating star JoJo Starbuck (it is on-again-off-again at this time), and through criticisms in the press that he was just an immensely talented but dumb athlete. And when the Steelers would lose, he'd be booed and feel mortally wounded.

He came to the Steelers out of tiny Louisiana Tech, as a somewhat naive and overly protected number one draft pick. A blond, handsome, well-built specimen, he could throw a football nearly the length of the field. He had been a champion javelin thrower as well, setting a national high school record. He came to a pro team that had been lackluster, to say the least, for most of its existence. The Steelers had never won a single NFL championship.

Well, after Bradshaw's first season, he wound up setting an NFL record—for interceptions thrown! Twenty-four of them.

And when he came onto the field, the lusty steel-mill Pittsburgh fans booed the drawling Li'l Abner quarterback.

"Before a game then," he recalled, "I would get scared. I felt it in the pit of my stomach. I didn't sleep. I didn't eat. I didn't play well. It was a horrible nightmare."

But Bradshaw fought the crowds, fought the opponents, fought himself, and prevailed.

"Now he goes into a game with a different attitude than he had back then," says Dick Hoak, Steelers' offensive backfield coach. "You can tell by the way he warms up. Now he says, 'We're going out there and throw that sucker.' Three or four years ago he wouldn't even want to talk before a game, and if he did he'd say, 'What do we want to do?' "

In January 1980, despite all of the self-confidence he had developed over the last several years, Bradshaw was disturbed by the fear that his heavily favored Steelers would be upset by the Rams in the Super Bowl.

"Everything was pointing toward disaster," Terry says now.

In an article by Malcolm Moran in *Sport Magazine,* the improbable scenario was explained by Bradshaw:

"It all began when Bradshaw and Mike Kruczek, then the Steeler backup quarterback, saw the movie *Heaven Can Wait.* It tells the story of a man who is called to Heaven by mistake and then comes back to Earth as a quarterback for the Los Angeles Rams, eventually leading the Rams to a Super Bowl victory over the Steelers.

"Terry was nagged by the fear that life would copy art.

" 'I'm surprised that they didn't have the movie on our sets in the hotel room,' Terry says. There were also real-life facts: three Ram assistant coaches had once been Steelers, and knew the Steeler system; rain had turned the practice field to slop; Bradshaw thought his practices were poor. But when the Rams were in position for an upset, Bradshaw threw too late, long touchdown passes for a dramatic 31–19 Steeler win."

After the game, Bradshaw talked of quitting within two years, but then recanted and said he'd play until he was 38—he is now 32.

However, after the 1980 season, there was talk

of retirement again.

Bradshaw, who had played a role in the movie *Hooper* with Burt Reynolds, cut a country and western album and had a few club dates with his singing idol, Larry Gatlin. More importantly, he was involved in a television series pilot. His agent, David Gershenson, said from his Los Angeles office, "Terry's football career would probably come to an end if NBC agreed to purchase the series. The agreement calls for Terry to star in a pilot. If that happens, it will go into production right away. Terry won't be able to play football. Only if NBC doesn't pick up the series will Terry be available to play." The program, called "Short Trackers," is about a two-man auto-racing team.

Bradshaw confirmed Gershenson's remarks. But Joe Gordon, public relations director for the Steelers, said Bradshaw had another year on his contract and that he'd be surprised if Bradshaw retired.

So would the rest of the football world. It is unlikely that, when the dust of last season has settled, and Bradshaw has a good look back, he will quit. Football is still much in his blood, and he still possesses great football power.

On the other hand, he has learned to be his own man. "I guess you develop a hard crust," he said. "You almost have to to survive." Whether we see him in a football uniform again or not, Terry Bradshaw has provided us with enough thrills to last us a very long time.

Earl Campbell

IT WAS SUPPOSED TO HAVE been the Houston Oilers' year. After disappointments in the last few play-offs, many experts expected them to get to the Super Bowl and win it. Changes—particularly at quarterback, with Ken Stabler being traded for Dan Pastorini—were made. But the most compelling part of the team remained, of course. That was Earl Campbell.

It is *always* Earl's year. And 1980 proved it again.

For the third straight season in as many years in the league, Campbell led the NFL in rushing, this time by nearly 500 yards. He fell just 69 yards short of O. J. Simpson's season rushing record (2,003), finishing with 1,934 yards. Campbell also had the best average per rush, 5.2 yards.

His coach for the last three years—or ever since he joined the Oilers from the University of Texas—Bum Phillips, says, "Earl may not be in a class by himself, but it doesn't take long to call the roll."

Phillips and Campbell have been close with a

mutual respect and a kind of father-son relationship binding them. Campbell, like others, knew that if the Oilers did not have a Super Bowl-bound team, Bum might not be around in 1981.

Houston made it to the play-offs as a wild-card entry, and played Oakland in the first game. The Oilers lost, 27–7, as the Raiders put up a remarkable defense. It took every ounce of Campbell's great ability to gain his 91 yards in 27 carries.

As some people had thought, Bum Phillips was fired shortly after the beating by the Raiders.

Now, Bum was well-liked by many, not only because he is a fine football coach, but because he is a unique character, famous for his one-liners. Phillips, who wears a white, ten-gallon hat and cowboy boots, and chews tobacco on the sidelines, was once sent a pair of $500 armadillo-skin boots by an admirer. A reporter asked Bum if that wasn't a lot of money for footwear. Bum agreed. "For $500," he admitted, "you could hire a guy to carry you."

One of Bum's favorite targets for his lines was his star running back, Campbell. Told that Earl Campbell seems to get up slowly after being tackled, Phillips replied, "Yeah, but he goes down slow too."

And Campbell, apparently, wasn't going to take Bum's firing lying down either.

Within a day of Phillips's firing, Campbell made a demand of the Oilers' front office: "If you don't pay me more money, then trade me." He said he wanted to renegotiate his contract—only one year after signing a $3 million, six-year agreement renegotiated from a previous contract.

Earl Campbell

"Money wasn't the prime objective—although it's always nice to have," wrote Gene Roswell, in the *New York Post.*

"It was, as close friends point out, Campbell's emotional response to the loss of Bum that sparked the ultimatum."

Roswell pointed out that Campbell was raised in a heavily matriarchal atmosphere—strong mother, no father—and his close relationship with the coach filled the void.

"Earl took Bum's dismissal hard," one source revealed. "His mother raised him to believe in the fundamentals of God, family ties, and loyalty. Bum did a lot for Earl and they grew real close.

"It's a strong father-son type relationship and now it's been broken up and Earl is just confused, angry, and resentful. You saw how he played his heart out for Bum, the punishment he took and the pain he ignored.

"I don't know who put the words in his mouth or what numbers they are asking ($1 million a year), but I know it's got to be somebody else behind the move. Earl basically just wants to go with Bum and maybe thinks this is one way of getting Bud Adams (Houston Oiler owner) to trade him."

Such an idea was immediately dismissed by club spokesman Mike McClure, who stated that the Oilers had no intention of dealing Campbell. The Luv Ya Blue fans (that is, Oiler diehards) were mad enough losing Bum, but the invasion of the Normandy coast would be nothing compared to the anger of the Houston mobs if Campbell were sent away.

"Maybe," the same source said, "the people here love Bum, and they hated to see him go, especially the way it was handled. (Bum heard the news on a TV newscast.) But they can handle that—have to. But in Houston, Texas, Earl Campbell is a god. Texas-born, Texas-raised. One of the greatest running backs who ever played the game."

Another friend of Campbell's said, "I guess he feels betrayed, so he's sloppin' it on them."

"There are no loopholes in his contract," said Campbell's agent, Will Stewart. "The Oilers can renegotiate Earl's contract, trade him, or Earl Campbell can't play pro football for the next five years."

There is no question that Earl Campbell will play pro football next year. The best bet as to the circumstances is that there will be a compromise in the renegotiation factor, and Earl Campbell will be making more money than his current contract calls for.

Returning to Campbell's relationship with Phillips, the pair came together in 1978 after Campbell finished his final season at Texas, in which he was named Heisman Trophy winner as best college football player in the nation. Phillips had been the Oiler head coach for three years, and the team had not made it to the play-offs. With Campbell, the Oiler chances would be increased considerably.

For years the Oiler running game had barely existed. The offense had consisted mostly of Pastorini cranking it up and throwing deep to Kenny Burrough, except when Pastorini was being buried under a ton of beef.

A joke around Houston at the time said that Oiler coaches had finally figured out the problem. The backs had been tipping their plays. Each time they broke from the huddle, one would be laughing and the other would be pale as a ghost.

"Then came the powerful and explosive Campbell and it was time for the other team to turn pale," as Mickey Herskowitz, a Houston sports columnist, described it.

Campbell was actually available for Tampa Bay to draft, but Phillips worked a deal in which the Oilers were able to get Campbell as their first-round draft pick.

In Campbell's first year, 1978, the Oilers reached the AFC championship game, losing to the Steelers in what Phillips described as "a knock at the door."

The next year they were back again. One step from the Super Bowl game. This time, in Bum's words, "banging at the door." And against Pittsburgh again.

And the Oilers lost again, 27–13. For Campbell, it was his worst day as a pro. He managed an average of 0.9 yards a carry, when he had been averaging 4. He gained only 15 yards in 17 carries. He was stopped behind the line of scrimmage five times and stopped five more times after gains of only one yard.

"We had them studied so well," Pittsburgh defensive end Dwight White said, "that our scouting report was as thick as an encyclopedia."

Did Campbell seek excuses for his performance? Was the groin injury that had bothered him in the latter part of the season a problem? Was his offensive line so inadequate that he could not get a chance to show his stuff? After all, this is the man whom a Denver linebacker once described this way: "What Earl does is pound you until you break, and then he breaks for one for 50 yards, and there he is in the end zone."

"No," said Campbell after the second Steeler-Oiler AFC title game, "I never felt faster. The traction was good—the ground crew did a good job getting the field in shape (Pittsburgh had experienced a heavy snowfall prior to the game). The problem was the Steelers. They never let me get started."

This past season, though, the Oilers derived some sense of revenge when, in the 14th game of the season, they whipped the Steelers 6–0 in Houston, and virtually wiped out Pittsburgh's chances of making the play-offs and going for a fifth Super Bowl title.

Campbell had found his running game against Pittsburgh and crashed for 81 yards in 21 carries, the best running statistics of anyone in the game. Second best was Pittsburgh's outstanding Franco Harris, who managed 54 yards in 16 carries. But it was another great defensive struggle and neither team could score a touchdown. The game was decided on two field goals—one each in the third and fourth quarters—by Oiler Toni Fritsch.

Campbell saved one of his best performances of the season for the following game, against Green Bay, in which a win would assure the Oilers of a play-off spot. Inspired by playing at Lambeau Field, where the Vince Lombardi legend was shaped, he ran for two touchdowns and for 181 yards and surpassed his single-season rushing best in the Oilers' 22–3 win.

"All that's fine," Campbell said of his rushing feats. "When I get out of football, I'm going to have a chance to look back over my years and really appreciate it. But as far as it stands now, I don't think it's fun until you can do that (win rushing titles) and make it to the big game, the Super Bowl, and then win that one.

Campbell recalled the first NFL game he attended—Green Bay at Dallas—at age 13. Lombardi was the Packer coach and Bart Starr was their quarterback.

Starr is now the Packers' coach and Campbell shook his hand. "I told him that it was a pleasure to meet him, that he was the first quarterback I saw play pro football in person, that it was kind of a pleasure to play where so many legends have played," Campbell said.

As for Lombardi, Campbell remembered, "I guess Vince Lombardi was a guy like myself, always liked to work, work, work."

Walter Payton

THIS IS HOW IT GOES for the Chicago Bears: On their very best day of the 1980 season, in which they walloped the Green Bay Packers 61–7 (you read it right), they suffered their most grievous loss—a chance for the play-offs.

In their 14th game of a 16-game schedule—in which they scored their biggest victory in 15 years—the Bears sadly noted that Minnesota had also beaten Tampa Bay, which eliminated the Bears from a play-off berth in the Central Division of the National Football Conference.

"It's very disappointing," said the Bears' star running back Walter Payton.

All Payton had done that afternoon was run for three touchdowns (including the first two scores of the game), and totaled 130 yards gained rushing.

Disappointing? Well, two weeks later, after the last game of the season, against Tampa Bay, in which he again ran for 130 yards, and won his record fifth straight rushing title in the NFC, he said, "None of it's important if you don't make the play-offs."

The play-offs, and, at the end of the rainbow, the glittering Super Bowl ring, is a great motivating factor in the life of every pro football player. None more so than Walter Payton, a perennial all-star, and, now, fifth on the list of all-time NFL rushers, with 8,386 yards gained. (Only Jim Brown, O. J. Simpson, Jim Taylor, and Franco Harris are ahead of him.)

But only twice in his six seasons have the Bears made the play-offs, and both times they were eliminated in the first round, losing to Dallas 37–7 in 1977, and to Philadelphia 27–17 in 1979.

That he can't lead his team further is no reflection on his abilities, of course, but on the cast of characters that management surrounds him with. Yet the frustration is there.

Payton says, "I want to leave the game with people saying, 'Now that Walter Payton, he was a team player.'"

And, needless to say, "a winner."

He is as fidgety to win as he was the afternoon that a reporter spotted him on the practice field. The Bears are practicing field goals and it is obvious that Payton is not comfortable sitting.

So he jumps up and he picks up a ball and stands under the goal posts. As the kicks sail over his head, he flings the ball at each passing kick. He hits them nearly every time.

That is some feat, but his teammates hardly notice. After all, these people have seen Walter Payton perform even more incredible things—like darting through entire teams to score touchdowns.

In some ways, too many people have not noticed him. He makes it look so easy, like when he

Walter Payton, Leading Rusher in the NFC

makes an eight-yard gain that perhaps should have been only a two-yarder.

"The guy's amazing," said Bear free safety Doug Plank. "You'd think you'd get tired of saying it after awhile, but you don't. Week after week I see him put his head down and hit guys in the chest, and they get carried off. His ability to come up with a big play each week is amazing. Not just 70-yard runs, either. Five or six yards when maybe a little extra gets you a first down. Even if he isn't breaking long ones, he's doing things nobody else could have done."

One of those things caused him much anguish. It happened in the play-off game against the Eagles, on the Bears first play of the second half. The Bears held a 17–10 lead. They had just forced the Eagles to run three plays and punt, and the Bears took over on their 15. The next play called for a pitchout to the right to Payton. The success of the play depends on the perfectly executed block by the flanker (Brian Baschnagel, in this case) on the strong-side line backer (John Bunting). Baschnagel worked it brilliantly, going in motion to his right, drifting past Bunting, then cutting back and wiping him out.

Then Payton could find daylight, which is precisely what happened. And he dashed 84 yards down the sidelines before being knocked out of bounds on the 1-yard line. The Bears were sure to score again, and possibly clinch the game. However, back downfield, at the line of scrimmage, a yellow flag had been tossed by the referee signaling a penalty.

What now? Payton wondered. He soon found out. Baschnagel apparently had been overzealous in his block and was called for illegal motion.

Payton disagreed. "I don't think Brian did anything illegal," he said. But the all-pro back didn't fume, he didn't complain. He admitted, however, that "when you have a big play like that, and then a questionable call is made, it does take some of the wind out."

It took enough of the starch out of the Bears that they didn't score again, and Philadelphia did; two TD's and a field goal. And the disappointed Bears were eliminated from the play-offs.

At this time, Walter remembered the words of his mother during another period of disappointment for him. At their home in Columbia, Mississippi, she told him, "Son, don't worry about it. It was God's will. It was probably the best thing for you that it happened as it did. Because now you have a target to shoot at."

It is this level-headed philosophy that sometimes obscures the achievements of Payton. In an age when the public is hungry for the outrageous, Payton is simply superior. He doesn't covet the spotlight, like many celebrities. When he begins an interview, he asks, "How long will it take?" He prefers to let his work on the field do his talking, but when he must talk, he prefers to talk, naturally, on the run.

"One thing, and one thing only, makes Walter Payton tick," says his agent, Bud Holmes, "and that's competition."

"He's one of the guys from the old school who sticks his nose in there," said Rick Casares, whose Bears' career rushing records have been broken by Payton. That's one more way Payton is a throwback. He's a good enough athlete to play every down. He makes a better newsreel clip than talk show guest, and, as Casares says, he sticks his nose right into the thick of things.

"You know, during my career, I don't think there were ten times I ever went out of bounds," Casares said. "The goal line's down at the other end of the field, not on the sideline. I'd be embarrassed the way most of those guys run out of bounds today. But Payton runs up that field. He doesn't just go through the motions."

According to Chicago sportswriter Kevin Lamb, "Fans fear for Payton's safety because of that style of running, arms and legs flailing, daring tacklers to hit him one more time or watch him escape. After 1,965 carries in his first six years, they have begun to more appropriately fear for the people trying to tackle him."

As Payton explains, that was always his idea. "If you want to play a long time," he said, "you have to protect yourself. You can't always keep accepting the blows."

Gale Sayers understands this philosophy. Sayers, the Bears' breakaway runner before Payton, says, "What people don't realize is that speed is power. Walter is only 5-10, 200 pounds, small compared to some of those 6-6, 300-pound linemen; but if you are a good, quick runner, and you have the speed, and you hit somebody, then you're going to hurt that somebody."

Payton carries the philosophy of self-defense to the point where Bears' offensive lineman Ted Albrecht says, "Sometimes he comes back to the huddle and he wants to know if he punished the guy who tackled him."

Payton goes into orbit for a TD against Green Bay.

His strength is what sets him apart from most other running backs. He has limbs and a torso that seem perfectly tailored for a hard-driving running back. One does not tackle him with a single pair of arms.

"Maybe barbed wire," suggests Vikings cornerback Bobby Bryant. "I figure it's similar to trying to rope a calf. It's hard enough to get your hands on him, and once you do, you wonder if you should have."

"He's so darn aggressive out there," says New York Jets offensive tackle Marvin Powell. "He's shifty, and can run around you, but I get the impression that he'd just as soon run over you. And leave a few cleat marks on your chest as his calling card."

Bears General Manager Jim Finks says Payton already is the finest running back in the history of the game. Quite a statement, but allowances are made for personal prejudice. However, Bear head coach Neill Armstrong adds another dimension to the encomiums for Payton. "I have not seen a running back in the NFL who blocks as well as he does."

He's also an excellent pass catcher—and he can throw the ball. Against Minnesota in 1979, he snared a pitchout, and instead of barreling ahead, he stopped and threw a 54-yard touchdown pass.

"He can do anything with a football," said teammate Plank.

"Payton scares me to death," said Detroit coach Monte Clark.

"We all know that Walter Payton is the Chicago Bears," said Jim Trimble, the Giants' former player personnel director.

That is precisely the kind of viewpoint that gets

under Payton's skin. He goes through a lot of trouble to get offensive linemen to spike the ball when he scores the touchdown, dragging them in front of television cameras with him, taking credit collectively instead of individually, gesturing with palms down for the fans to stop when they are booing one of the Bears. You see, Payton wants to be known as the team player, the ultimate company man.

But he is also the ultimate paradox. He blends smoothly with the team—by design—yet rises above it, despite himself.

Vince Ferragamo

"HE HAS AN ARM LIKE a bullwhip, a face hijacked from a schoolgirl's dream," began an article in *Inside Sports* magazine. "He has teeth that line up like ivory soldiers and deep black hair that looks good even when the wind is done with it.

"He has the glamour center of the world for his playground, moviemakers and ad agencies on the fringe of his huddle.

"He has an offensive line that gives the bullwhip time to flick and sting. He has statistics that are shinier than any quarterback's in the league. He has a 15-for-25 Super Bowl in his dossier, in the eighth game he ever started in the National Football League.

"If you could be anyone in the world right now, Vince Ferragamo would not be a bad choice."

But hold on. Nothing is ever as it seems. And in the case of Vince Ferragamo, there is a fly in the ointment of grandeur, a caterpillar in the salad of delight.

Respect. Admiration. Salary commensurate with

his stature and accomplishments. All these, Vince felt, were not forthcoming from those who mattered most, Vince's employers, the Los Angeles Rams.

And thereby hangs the tale of this tarnished Golden Boy.

Go back to November of 1979. Vince Ferragamo, a 6-3, 212-pound 25-year-old, had spent most of the last three seasons as a second- and third-string quarterback. As a fourth-round draft choice from the University of Nebraska in 1977, he had never been given much of an opportunity in the pros. Now in the tenth game of the season, against Seattle, Ferragamo is called into action. Starting quarterback Pat Haden suffers a freak accident. The little finger of his passing (right) hand breaks when it catches in the seam of the artificial turf.

Ferragamo comes on to lead the Rams to a victory, throwing two touchdowns in a 20–14 win.

Before the Seattle game, the Rams had a 5–6 record and prospects for the play-offs appeared dreary. With Ferragamo at quarterback, the Rams won four out of their next five games and met the Dallas Cowboys in the first round of the play-offs.

At Texas Stadium the Rams were expected to be eliminated from the play-offs again—they had been knocked out in play-offs in each of the six preceding years. But Ferragamo threw three long touchdown passes—including one 55 yards in the air, while being clobbered by Randy White—and the Rams whipped the Cowboys.

Then, January 6, at Tampa Stadium, an even more poised Ferragamo threw for 163 yards as the Rams, implementing a planned ball-control offense, won the National Football Conference title from the Tampa Bay Buccaneers, 9–0.

Next, the Super Bowl. On the day before the 1980 title game in which the Rams were up against the Pittsburgh Steelers, the *New York Times* wrote what many people were saying and thinking:

"The main difference between the Pittsburgh Steelers and the Los Angeles Rams would seem to be at quarterback. (That is, Terry Bradshaw versus Vince Ferragamo.) The winning quarterbacks in the previous Super Bowls have been named Bart Starr, Joe Namath, Len Dawson, Johnny Unitas, Earl Morrall, Roger Staubach, Bob Griese, Ken Stabler, and for a record three times, Terry Bradshaw.

"There is not a Vince Ferragamo in that bunch."

Why that sentiment? Several times in the games he had started, Ram coach Ray Malavasi had "jerked" Ferragamo out of the game. He was in-experienced, was one rap; he didn't follow the coach's orders, was another.

It seemed the only person not worrying about Ferragamo's Super Bowl performance was Ferragamo himself. "I've satisfied myself," he said. "I know I can play. And I'll prove it in the Super Bowl."

Which is precisely what he did. He completed 15 of 25 passes for 212 yards, nearly devastating the Steelers with his downfield passing game. He read blitzes. He showed exceptional poise.

He threw just one interception, compared with Bradshaw's three, but that one turned the game around. The Rams were down 24–19 in the fourth quarter, and on the move. They got to the Steel-ers' 31. On first down, the Ram coaches sent in a play; pass up the middle. Ferragamo dropped back, spotted receiver Ron Smith, and let fly. But defender Jack Lambert darted in and picked off the pass. The Steelers took possession, and several plays later scored to ice the game.

Regardless, Malavasi said that Vince "was great, just great. For a third-year guy, I can't believe how well he threw the ball against a defense like Pittsburgh's. He showed me a lot of character today."

By the opening of the following season, however, the Super Bowl star (he was second to Bradshaw in the voting for Most Valuable Player in the game), Vince Ferragamo, was again playing second-string quarterback to Pat Haden.

Ferragamo was displeased, to say the least, but he bit the bullet. In the Rams' first game against the Detroit Lions, Haden oddly enough broke his passing hand *again,* and Ferragamo came on again to save the Rams.

It should be noted, however, that the relationship between quarterbacks Haden and Ferragamo became strained, at best.

Says Haden: "Vince is maybe feeling some pressures I always felt in my Ram career, that there's somebody over your shoulder."

Says Ferragamo: "Why should I feel sorry for him? When Pat was No. 1, I don't think he felt empathy or sympathy for me. I remember how I was treated as a second-string quarterback. Like I was lucky that they let me hang around. I'll never forget it."

The personalities involved are obviously different. Haden at 27 is only a year older than Ferragamo but considerably less temperamental. Ferragamo is brash, high-strung. Both are handsome, intelligent, well-spoken. Haden is a former Rhodes scholar now working on his law degree. Ferragamo started studying medicine a year ago but interrupted it after winning the Rams' first-string assignment.

As forceful, competitive personalities, both have an aversion to being number two. As starters, each guarded his domain like a watchdog.

On November 2, after Ferragamo had thrown five touchdown passes in a romp over New Orleans, the Rams sent in a now-mended Haden to give Ferragamo a rest. Ferragamo fumed on the sidelines. "They never put me in during the third quarter," he said, referring to his days of clipboard holding while Haden did the quarterbacking.

Ferragamo, though, remained the uncontested first-string quarterback, and led the Rams to an 11–5 season and, again, a meeting with the Dallas Cowboys in the first round of the play-offs. This time, the Cowboys won, as they put tremendous rushing pressure on Ferragamo. Final score, Dallas 34, LA 13.

Despite this, Ferragamo had a sensational season. He was statistically the second-best quarterback in the National Football Conference (losing out in the complicated ratings system to Ron Jaworski by a mere percentage point). He led, though, in touchdown passes (30), percentage of passes for touchdowns (7.4) and average yards gained passing (almost 8).

For most of the season, Ferragamo was battling his employers about as much as he was the rest of the NFL's defensive linemen. He makes $52,000 a year, peon's wages for an NFL quarterback. Haden, for example, pulls down $200,000 a year, and makes more in endorsements than Ferragamo does in salary.

Ferragamo played hookey from practice to underscore his contract demands. This was just three days before a game with Tampa Bay. Ferragamo's Beverly Hills attorney, Paul Caruso, said that the reluctant hero would not play without a new contract. The Rams said OK, let's sit down. A week later, after Caruso negotiated a $750,000 agreement for his client, Ferragamo abruptly fired Caruso and said he was taking over the contract talks himself.

The Rams then said that they would not discuss contract until the season ended. Since they didn't come to an agreement, Ferragamo became a free agent.

Early in the spring Ferragamo announced that he was negotiating with the Montreal Alouettes, and in April he signed with the Canadian team.

As for the Rams' starting quarterback next year—well, Ferragamo had been successful, of course, but so had Haden. (In the 43 games Haden has started, the Rams are 30-12-1.)

"This is a club that has won with a variety of quarterbacks," Ram general manager Don Klosterman had said. "Now, we *did* get to a Super Bowl last year—but a lot of people contributed. We thought the world of Vince Ferragamo. But this is an ideal club for a quarterback.

"Fifteen games don't make a quarterback. Vince is an outstanding talent, but in sports there are roller-coaster careers, not that this is one."

That was hardly a vote of confidence.

Haden has said, "I want to play very, very badly. I hate sitting on the bench."

He may get his chance in September.

II
RAMBLING
TO PAYDIRT!

NFC
Championship
Philadelphia 20, Dallas 7
Veterans Stadium, Philadelphia
Sunday, January 11, 1981

USUALLY UNEMOTIONAL TOM LANDRY, THE
Dallas coach, stood on the sidelines near the end
of the game and grimaced—a fairly shocking facial
expression for Landry. In fact, any facial expression other than his Great Stone Face would be
shocking. He had on a round fur hat with ear flaps
on this miserably cold afternoon that saw temper-
atures dip to 17 degrees. Was he grimacing because the chilling weather had got to him or because his Cowboys were going down to defeat?

Whatever, it was just another of the many
small—and large—dramas that unfolded in this
championship game. Perhaps the most significant
was that surrounding Philadelphia's two starting
running backs, Wilbert Montgomery and Leroy
Harris—"two hungry young gents with Phi Beta
Kappa feet," wrote Red Smith, the esteemed *New
York Times* sports columnist.

"Montgomery, a greyhound with muscles, and
Harris who runs like an infuriated beer truck,
ripped through and around the Dallas defenses for

*Leroy Harris Turning the Corner for a Big
Gainer*

the points that qualified the Eagles for Super Bowl XV two weeks hence," added Smith.

Before the game, Montgomery was a doubtful participant, let alone a starter, let alone the potential game hero.

The pain in his left knee was bad. On the day before the title game, he had limped painfully through workouts. Three days before that his knee had collapsed during practice. He had twisted his knee in a previous game, and had missed four complete games this season, had come back prematurely—and had sat out the better part of three others.

If there is a way for Wilbert Montgomery to play, however, he will play. The game opened and Montgomery was dressed out, but on the sidelines. On the Eagles' second play from scrimmage, he was called in. He came running toward the huddle.

On the very next play, the Eagles' slight halfback (5-9, 165 pounds) took a handoff from Ron Jaworski, the quarterback, started up the middle, veered toward a hole at left tackle, leaned heavily on his wobbly left knee and cut sharply to his right without ever tapping the brakes to whiz 42 yards to the end zone. And the first score of the day.

Wilbert Montgomery never stopped running after that. He had the greatest game of his life, gaining 194 yards on 26 carries. He came within only 2 yards of the NFL play-off rushing record, set by Philadelphia's Steve Van Buren against the Rams in 1946, eight years before Montgomery was born.

Harris, meanwhile, had 60 yards gained and had scored one touchdown, like Montgomery.

Barefoot Kicker Tony Franklin

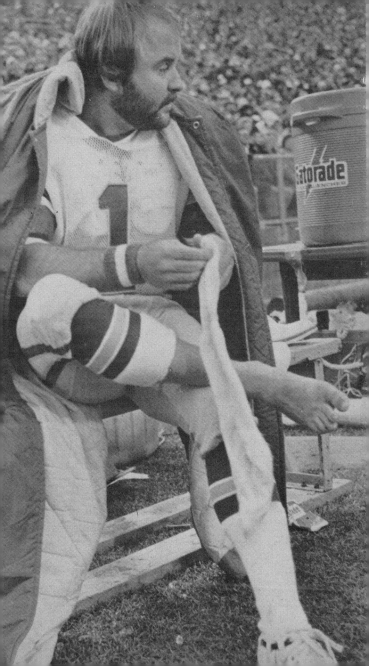

Tony Franklin, the barefoot soccer-style kicker, added two field goals and two extra points, and the Eagles had run up 20 points. Tony Dorsett's three-yard run and Rafael Septien's extra point were the only scoring by the Cowboys.

Montgomery's first run set the tone of the game. The Cowboys, expecting a pass from the way the Eagles' offense lined up, was completely fooled by the run.

"We caught them," said Philadelphia coach Dick Vermeil.

But the Cowboys came back with a solid 68-yard TD drive to tie the score in the second period, a drive that saw Tony Dorsett and Robert Newhouse, the two running backs, gain big yards on running plays.

It would be the only time in the game in which Dallas dominated play. It held the ball for six minutes on the drive and the Dallas offense virtually had free rein over the Eagles defense.

The Eagles were frustrated several times in the first half. They couldn't score again. They kept taking the ball right up to the goal line but something always seemed to happen. Once, Franklin missed a field goal. Another time, there was a high snap on a fake field goal. It all added up to a 7–7 tie at the intermission.

As the third quarter began, it was anybody's ball game. But then Dallas began to fray at the seams.

"The key to the whole game was the third quarter," said Dallas coach Landry. "We turned the ball over three times. We had a chance to win at halftime and I thought we would win. We just had to play well and avoid turnovers, which we didn't."

Danny White tries to bring Dallas back.

In the third period, the Cowboys' James Jones dropped a punt reception, but the fumble turned out not to hurt the Cowboys.

The next one created damage. Dallas quarterback Danny White was sacked by Carl Hairston, fumbled the ball and lost it, paving the way for Tony Franklin's 26-yard field goal, and a 10–7 Eagles lead.

A 28-yard pass from White to Jay Saldi next took the Cowboys to the Eagles' 32. Then Tony Dorsett fumbled and Jerry Robinson picked up the loose ball and ran it back 22 yards to the Dallas 38. Two plays later, Harris took the ball in for a touchdown.

The fourth quarter had no fireworks, which was surprising, considering how Dallas often pulls games out of a hat as if by magic. The Eagles added 3 points on a 20-yard field goal by Franklin at the end of a 62-yard drive that used up almost seven minutes of playing time. There was no other scoring.

Said Danny White afterward, "We never got things going and Philadelphia's defense had a lot to do with that. They were outstanding—defense and offense. They played a tremendous game."

AFC
Championship
Oakland 34, San Diego 27
San Diego Stadium, San Diego
Sunday, January 11, 1981

THE FIRST SET OF DOWNS ended in a crazy touchdown pass. And the second set of downs ended in only a somewhat less-zany touchdown pass.

From then on, the game settled down into the normal frenzy known and loved by fans of National Football League play.

And when it was over, the Oakland Raiders, the most improbable of title contenders, had earned their way to their third Super Bowl, while the San Diego Chargers would have to wait another year before they could hope to get to their first.

The Raiders started the year with a 2–3 record and a retread quarterback, Jim Plunkett. Plunkett's knee and shoulder were scarred by surgery and his psyche hurt from years as a loser. He was traded by the Patriots, put on waivers by the 49ers, and ignored for more than two seasons by the Raiders. And throw in a few hundred sacks along the way. Yet this same Jim Plunkett led the crazy wild-card Raiders into the Super Bowl.

On the third play from scrimmage, Plunkett dropped back to pass and threw a short one over the middle on third down with 4 yards to go. The pass hit Kenny King, the running back and intended receiver, and popped into the air behind him. It was grabbed by Raymond Chester, the tight end. Ray Preston, a San Diego linebacker who had headed toward King, went past Chester too late to slow down, and Chester completed a bizarre 65-yard touchdown.

The play reminded many observers of one in 1972, when the Raiders were eliminated from the play-offs on a deflected pass caught by Franco Harris of Pittsburgh, that was quickly dubbed "The Immaculate Reception."

The ball changed hands a few times after ensuing punts. Then Dan Fouts, San Diego quarterback, lofted a 48-yard pass into the center of the end zone. Charlie Joiner, the wide receiver, outleaped Mike Davis, the safety, and grabbed the ball, but it bobbled out of his hands and bounced on his helmet before he grabbed it for another rather odd touchdown pass play.

It was 7–7, and still in the first half. A pass interference penalty against Preston led to the second Oakland touchdown.

Preston was matched against Todd Christensen, a Raiders running back who was going down the right sideline. The penalty put the ball at the San Diego 12. Three plays later, Plunkett, weak knees and all, scrambled 5 yards into the end zone for a 14–7 lead.

Plunkett, passing deftly on another downfield charge, finished this one with a 21-yard pass to King, and the Raiders lead widened to 21–7.

But the Raiders still weren't through scoring in this half. Plunkett's 24-yard pass to Cliff Branch set up a run by Mark van Eeghan for a 3-yard TD plunge.

The Chargers' Charlie Joiner caught his second touchdown pass of the game, and the Chargers' second touchdown—and 8-yard pass from Fouts— shortly before the second period closed. Despite much scoring by both teams, at the close of the first half the Raiders held a surprisingly strong 28-14 lead.

Many expected the San Diego Chargers to make a formidable showing in the second half, particularly on offense.

After all, the Chargers were the strongest offensive team in the AFC, especially in the area of passing. They were tops in the league with 283.2 yards gained passing per game, and Fouts with 24 TD passes had led the conference.

And indeed the Chargers made their move right after the second-half kickoff.

They got down to the Raiders' 8-yard line. Then, on second down, John Jefferson broke clear in the end zone, and the great receiver was waving for the ball. When the ball arrived, however, it deflected off him, bounced high behind him, and went out of bounds.

On third down, Jefferson, who is considered the finest pass catcher perhaps in all of football, failed in a leaping attempt to catch another Fouts pass, and the Chargers reluctantly settled for a 26-yard field goal by Rolf Benirschke.

Oakland 28, San Diego 17.

The Raiders were stopped, and a 28-yard return of a Ray Guy punt by Mike Fuller gave San Diego

the ball at the Oakland 41. The Chargers, gaining momentum, drove toward a touchdown.

Chuck Muncie, the San Diego running back who returned to the game despite an injured shoulder, followed the guard Doug Wilkerson on a 6-yard sweep to the left corner of the end zone, and the score became 28–24 midway in the third period.

"We knew there was no way of stopping that San Diego passing game [the Chargers netted 351 yards in the air]," said Oakland coach Tom Flores. "We felt they were going to get their share of passing yards. But our plan was to make them work for it. We wanted to make them drive the length of the field for their touchdowns. We didn't want to give up the big play. We didn't want to give them any turnovers, any cheap field position."

And the Raiders followed that plan perfectly.

The Raiders now hung on, with two Chris Bahr field goals and a tremendous 6-minute, 43-second closing stretch of ball control.

Bahr's field goals were from 27 and 33 yards out, the last came 5:14 into the fourth quarter.

With seven minutes left in the game, the Chargers had driven 72 yards in 12 plays, on passes from Fouts to Muncie for 17 and to Winslow for 21, and runs by Muncie of 11 and 16 yards. But they were stopped at the 27-yard line and they had to settle for a field goal by Benirschke, to make it 34–27 for Oakland.

It was the last real scoring opportunity for either team.

Ray Guy, Superb Oakland Punter

Super Bowl Review

IT HAS BEEN SUGGESTED THAT the Super
Bowl, because it has become such big business,
ought to be known as the "$uper Bowl."

According to the New Orleans Chamber of
Commerce, host for the 15th Super Bowl game,
some 70,000 visitors were drawn to the Crescent
City and left behind an estimated $40 million at,
among other places, the Louisiana Superdome,
New Orleans hotels, the world-famous restaurants,
and the bars and other night spots in the French
Quarter.

Thousands of fans or, in the case of large cor-
porations, their employees and clients, find it so
necessary to attend that they are willing to spend
as much as $500 for a $40 ticket.

The National Broadcasting Company finds it important enough to give the NFL $6 million for the
right to televise the game, and sponsors find it important enough to give NBC $275,000 for a
30-second commercial. "We had been sold out for
months before the game," an NBC spokesman

said, meaning NBC would take in $12,650,000 for the 23 minutes of commercial time available.

With this kind of money floating around, it seems that the players themselves are earning relative peanuts. Each winning player gets $18,000 for participating in the game, and each losing player $9,000. But, come to think of it, not bad for two hours' work on a Sunday afternoon.

The Super Bowl has come a long, long way from its rather humble beginnings—just 15 years ago.

The first one, held in the Memorial Coliseum in Los Angeles, was played before 30,000 empty seats. It has taken a little while for the game to develop into the huge media and corporate-prestige event it has become.

The Super Bowl was billed as a super spectacle right from the beginning. After the merger in 1966 of the two warring leagues—they both came under the aegis of the National Football League—the executives for the American Football Conference and the National Football Conference decided there should be a game to determine the world champions. *World,* of course, referred to just the United States.

Football Commissioner Pete Rozelle sought a catchy name for the championship game. Rozelle is a former public relations man for the Los Angeles Rams (and, before that, for the University of San Francisco) who became commissioner, first for the NFL in 1960, and then of the combined leagues. He is well aware of the impact of image.

Lamar Hunt, owner of the Kansas City Chiefs, had an idea. He had bought his little daughter a funny ball that bounced crazily around the house. She called it a "super ball." The phrase lodged in Hunt's mind. When suggestions for a name for the new title game were requested, Hunt offered "Super Bowl."

The committee agreed that the name was perfect. It had that simple, lofty, easily identifiable Madison Avenue ring to it.

The first championship between the leagues was set for January 15, 1967. The contestants were the powerful Green Bay Packers coached by Vince Lombardi and the Kansas City Chiefs led by coach Hank Stram. The Los Angeles Coliseum was the site.

The newer AFC was suffering a credibility gap. Few knew how good or how bad the teams from that conference were (it was barely ten years old). And, by extension, the players of the AFC were considered questionable.

"On the plane, somewhere between Kansas City and Los Angeles, I realized our team was scared to death," said Fred Williamson, left corner back for the Kansas City Chiefs. "I looked around and all I saw were zombies. These guys were scared of playing the Green Bay Packers in the first Super Bowl, scared of the unknown."

Just before the game, 4,000 pigeons were released into the air, for reasons known only to the NFL promotion department.

The game began as Mike Mercer kicked off for KC.

The Packers—led by Bart Starr, Paul Hornung, and Jerry Kramer—scored first, with Max McGee snaring a pass from Starr. Chiefs' quarterback Len Dawson's toss to Curtis McClinton tied it up. Then the Packers went on a binge and won the game going away in the second half. Final score: Green Bay 35, Kansas City 10.

Starr completed 16 of 23 passes for 250 yards and two touchdowns and won the Most Valuable Player award for the game.

The "Pack" was back in 1968 to face the Oakland Raiders, and the setting was the Orange Bowl in Miami.

Before the game, Lombardi told his troops, "Let me say just this: All the glory, everything that you've won, is going to be small in comparison to winning this game. This is the greatest thing for you. You're the only team maybe in the history of the National Football League to ever have this opportunity to win the Super Bowl twice. Boys, I tell you, I'd be so proud of that I'd just fill up with myself. I'd just get bigger and bigger."

The Packers indeed won, but Lombardi did not float like a balloon. The Packers were emotionally charged for this game. They knew it would be Lombardi's last as their coach. He would be stepping up to the front office. After the game, two of his players, Kramer and Forrest Gregg, carried him off the field on their shoulders.

In this game, as in the previous Super Bowl, Green Bay led by a small margin of nine points at the half and then came on strongly in the final two quarters to demonstrate their superiority.

Starr was named MVP for the second straight year, after hitting 13 of 24 passes for 202 yards and one TD. Don Chandler booted four field goals for Green Bay. The score: Packers 33, Raiders 14.

Henry Jordan of the Packers said: "The AFC's getting better. If they improve as much each year, they'll be on par with us soon."

How right he was. Super Bowl III proved it.

The Baltimore Colts of the NFC were 20-point favorites to beat Joe Namath and the New York Jets. In its first two encounters in championship play with the NFC, the AFC had very little to boast about.

This did not faze the Jets' pyrotechnical quarterback Namath. He told the Miami Touchdown Club luncheon a few days before the game, "We are going to win on Sunday. I guarantee it."

He asserted that the AFC had at least four quarterbacks superior to the Colts' Earl Morrall. As it turned out, Morrall did not have a particularly good day. And after a while the Colts had to call in their injured veteran star, John Unitas. But he could not set the Colts right, either.

The Jets calmly and quickly took charge. Known as a wide-open passing team, the Jets surprised many by establishing a tight ground game. Namath was a master field leader. He worked the fullback, Matt Snell, inside and outside; then, when Baltimore began to converge on Snell, Namath hit the Jet receivers, particularly George Sauer. New York won a major upset 16–7.

Snell gained 121 yards on 30 carries. Namath completed 17 of 28 passes for 206 yards and was named MVP.

This game made the Super Bowl a legitimate national sports attraction. And it also established the AFC as being on a par with the NFC. One other thing: It made Joe Namath the reigning folk hero of American sports.

To hype Super Bowl IV, the NFL and the TV network called the day of the game "Super Sunday." The contest between the Kansas City Chiefs and the Minnesota Vikings in New Orleans wasn't quite enough, the football people felt, so they added attractions before the game: 3,000 pigeons and 20,000 colored balloons were released into the air, and three tons of confetti were flung about.

A week before the game, fans were shocked to learn that quarterback Len Dawson's name had come up in a federal investigation of gambling. However, Dawson was cleared shortly before game time and he went on to lead the Chiefs to the AFC's second straight Super Bowl win, an easy 23–7 triumph over the Vikings.

The Chiefs took a 16–10 halftime lead by virtue of Dawson's ability to position his team so that Jan Stenerud could kick three field goals. Dawson completed 12 of 17 passes for 122 yards and was named MVP.

In Super Bowl V Jim O'Brien's field goal from the 32-yard line with five seconds left in the game gave the Baltimore Colts a victory over the Dallas Cowboys. The final score was 16–13. But the action was not nearly as dramatic as the score might indicate—there were 11 turnovers in the game, an embarrassingly high number for the two best teams in football.

It was, nonetheless, a satisfying win for the Colts, and particularly Morrall. It was a redemption of the loss to the Jets two years before.

Next it was Dallas's turn to redeem itself. Roger Staubach, Cowboy quarterback, passed and ran his team to a win over Miami in Super Bowl VI. The Dallas defense held Miami to just one field goal: Cowboys 24, Dolphins 3.

This was also the Super Bowl in which, for the first and only time in history, the President of the United States sent in a play. Richard Nixon called

Miami coach Don Shula a few nights before the game and suggested a pass play. It was a down-and-out pattern in which wide receiver Paul Warfield was supposed to catch the pass. The play was tried; it failed.

In Super Bowl VII, the Miami Dolphins were matched against the Washington Redskins. The Redskins were called the "Over-the-Hill Gang" because they had so many veteran players. The Dolphins, by contrast, were young and eager, and undefeated going into the game.

Miami played excellent football and led 14–0 with less than three minutes to play. Then Garo Yepremian, the Dolphins' Cyprus-born, soccer-style field-goal kicker, misplayed a field goal attempt and tried awkwardly to pass the ball. The pass was intercepted by Mike Bass and returned for Washington's only score.

The Dolphins, led by Larry Csonka, Bob Griese, and Manny Fernandez, had completed a perfect season—17–0—a pro football record.

The following year, in Super Bowl VIII, the Dolphins were back for their third straight appearance in the championship game. With an awesome display of power and skill they scored the first two times they had the ball, on marches of 62 and 56 yards, in the first quarter.

The Vikings could not score until the last quarter, when quarterback Fran Tarkenton ran the ball in from the 4-yard line. The final score was Miami 24, Minnesota 7. Csonka established two Super Bowl records in the game—most rushes, 33, and most yards gained, 145.

These records did not last long. Franco Harris of Pittsburgh broke them both the following year.

Running against the Vikings, again the NFC representative in the Super Bowl, Harris carried 34 times and gained 158 yards. And for the second straight year the Vikes were defeated in the title game. The score in Super Bowl IX was 16–6.

The Vikings had made it to the Super Bowl three times and had lost three times. It was also the third time the Vikings offense had been stymied by the opponents. The Steelers held Minnesota to just 119 yards total offense, including a Super Bowl low of 17 yards rushing. The Steelers, meanwhile, gained 333 yards.

In the following Super Bowl X, 80,187 fans jammed the Orange Bowl in Miami to watch the Steelers play the Cowboys. Pittsburgh won this one 21–17, for its second straight Super Bowl victory.

Highlights of the game were Terry Bradshaw's 64-yard pass for a touchdown to Lynn Swann, and an aggressive defense that snuffed out a late rally by the Cowboys. The final play was an end-zone interception by Glen Edwards of Pittsburgh.

Swann set a Super Bowl record in the game with four catches for 161 yards, and the Steelers set another record by sacking Staubach seven times. Franco Harris led rushers with 27 attempts for 82 yards. Bradshaw completed 9 of 19 passes for 209 yards.

In Super Bowl XI the Vikings were back in the glamour game for the fourth time—against the Oakland Raiders. It was Oakland's first appearance in the game since Super Bowl II. Once again the Vikings fell to defeat, this time by the wide margin of 32–14. A newspaper headline summed it up: "The Vikings: The Most Successful Failures."

Like most of the previous Super Bowl games, Super Bowl XII was a dismal failure artistically. Turnovers were the order of the day. Denver made more mistakes than Dallas did, and so succumbed to defeat, 27–10.

Denver turned the ball over eight times on fumbles and interceptions. Much credit, of course, had to be given to the Dallas defense, statistically rated the best in the NFC. Two Cowboy linemen—Harvey Martin and Randy White—shared the MVP award, which indicates where much of the credit for victory was due.

The game was very long. TV time-outs ran on and on (allowing the network to squeeze in as many commercials as possible). The halftime show ran on and on. And the change of quarters between the third and the fourth was perhaps the longest in history. The game took 3 hours and 32 minutes, a Super Bowl record.

"By the time we came out for the second half," said Dallas free safety Cliff Harris, "it seemed like a year had passed."

When the year in fact did pass, by calendar calculation, the Cowboys were back in the Super Bowl—this time against Pittsburgh. But Dallas didn't have the same luck it had had against Denver, and Tom Landry's well-oiled, highly mechanized team ran aground of the fine Steeler unit of Bradshaw, Harris, Swann, and the Pittsburgh defense in a dramatic Super Bowl XIII.

With less than two minutes to go and Pittsburgh ahead 35–17 by virtue of three touchdown passes by Terry Bradshaw (two to John Stallworth), Staubach led his Cowboy team back. They scored twice on drives of 89 and 52 yards. The last TD came with 22 seconds to go in the game, as the fans were howling with delight and suspense.

One more chance for Dallas. They would have to try an onside kick to regain possession of the ball. They tried it, but the kick landed in the hands of Pittsburgh's Rocky Bleier, and he fell on the ground at the Dallas 45. Bradshaw then ran out the clock.

Like lambs led to the slaughter, the Los Angeles Rams in Super Bowl XIV were expected to be wiped out by the Pittsburgh Steelers.

The prodigious Steelers were going after their fourth Super Bowl win, while the Rams had never been in the game before. The Steelers' 11–4 regular-season record tied for the best in football; the Rams' 9–7 mark was the worst of any team that ever made it to the Super Bowl.

The Rams at game time were 11-point underdogs.

Oddly enough, the Rams, with their surprisingly effective quarterback Vince Ferragamo (he started the season at second string), led the Steelers after the first quarter 7–3, and led at halftime 13–10. They were still leading the rough-tough Steelers after three quarters 19–17.

The Steelers in the fourth quarter seemed stymied. They had the ball on their 27-yard line, third down and eight. The situation demanded dramatics. Quarterback Terry Bradshaw provided them. Under a strong rush, Bradshaw threw the ball almost 50 yards downfield. John Stallworth caught it in full stride at the 32 and went in for the touchdown.

Later in the last quarter Franco Harris's 1-yard TD plunge added the frosting on the Steelers' 31–19 comeback win.

Super Bowl Summary

1967 at Los Angeles, Green Bay 35, Kansas
 City 10
1968 at Miami, Green Bay 33, Oakland 14
1969 at Miami, New York Jets 16, Baltimore 7
1970 at New Orleans, Kansas City 23,
 Minnesota 7
1971 at Miami, Baltimore 16, Dallas 13
1972 at New Orleans, Dallas 24, Miami 3
1973 at Los Angeles, Miami 14, Washington 7
1974 at Houston, Miami 24, Minnesota 7
1975 at New Orleans, Pittsburgh 16, Minnesota 6
1976 at Miami, Pittsburgh 21, Dallas 17
1977 at Pasadena, Oakland 32, Minnesota 14
1978 at New Orleans, Dallas 27, Denver 10
1979 at Miami, Pittsburgh 35, Dallas 31
1980 at Pasadena, Pittsburgh 31, Los Angeles 19
1981 at New Orleans, Oakland 27,
 Philadelphia 10

Super Bowl XV
Oakland 27, Philadelphia 10
Superdome, New Orleans
Sunday, January 25, 1981

A MAN GIVEN THE ASSIGNMENT of assembling a pro football team with the greatest assortment of has-beens, misfits, and rogues, would have come up with the Oakland Raiders. They were hardly a match made in heaven.

But they were heavenly.

Beginning the season with a 2 and 3 record, and losing their starting quarterback (one they had traded for in the off-season) to injury, they had managed to make the play-offs as a wild-card team. Then in four straight post-season games they were made the underdogs. And in four straight games they came out on top, the last game being the Super Bowl.

On the other hand—or on the opposite side of the field in the Super Bowl—the Philadelphia Eagles were a highly structured team who never missed curfews and were led by a strict disciplinarian named Dick Vermeil. In contrast, Oakland Raider Tom Flores had to run a looser ship. "If he suspended every one of his players who broke a

club rule," noted an observer, "he'd be the only one on the sidelines."

Their fans love the Raiders—they have had sell-out crowds for every game for years—but hate their owner, who is trying to move the team to Los Angeles. Their emblem is a man with a patch over one eye and two swords sticking out of his head.

The Eagles, in some ways projecting their own emblem—an eagle soaring with a football in its talons—sometimes seem to be above the battle. Their offense is a great aerial game dominated by Ron Jaworski—"The Polish Rifle" (a reference to his background and his exceptional throwing arm)—and 6-foot-8 pass-receiver Harold Carmichael.

In the end, though, it was the Raiders' quarterback, Jim Plunkett, who best symbolized the Raiders' victory. His was an old-fashioned success story—the revival of a 33-year-old quarterback who had lost his confidence after disappointing years with other teams. He was second-string when regular Dan Pastorini broke his leg in the fifth game of the season.

Plunkett threw three touchdown passes, including an 80-yarder—the longest play ever in a Super Bowl—to Kenny King that gave Oakland a decisive 14–0 lead with nine seconds to play in the opening quarter. The other two scoring passes went to Cliff Branch, one of the fun-loving Raiders who were disciplined in the week before the game. (In all, $15,000 in fines were levied by Flores on his players in the week they were in New Orleans.) Branch didn't even bother to call in sick when he missed a practice in midweek. No matter.

Back to Plunkett. He moved mechanically and

Ron Jaworski lets one fly over the outstretched arm of Raider Dave Browning.

completed 13 of 21 passes against the Eagles for 281 yards and was named the Most Valuable Player.

Meanwhile, Jaworski, the quarterback who produced much more impressive throwing statistics than Plunkett throughout the season, rarely had time to look for receivers. Plunkett's offensive line was giving him a full three seconds and more— very adequate time for a passer looking for his other ends—while Jaworski hardly was getting a second and a half to get his sights in order.

And when he did throw, it was not always to the right person. Three times he hit Rod Martin with sharp passes. The only problem was that Martin was playing for Oakland. Martin's three interceptions were a game and *career* record for the Super Bowl and helped turn the contest in favor of the Raiders. Oddly enough, Martin, another castoff— he had been cut by the 49ers and even the Raiders early in his career—had caught only two passes for the entire 1980 regular season.

On the third play of the game, Martin picked off his first pass on the Eagles' 46 and returned it 16 yards. Branch then caught a 14-yard pass and a 2-yard pass for the score. Chris Bahr, who kicked a pair of field goals, converted the first of his three extra points.

Martin's interception was the first hint that it wasn't going to be Jaworski's day. He completed a record-tying 18 passes for 291 yards, but he threw 38 times, to the almost total neglect of his running game. He could help his team across the goal line only once.

"I sensed a lack of emotion on our team before

Ted "The Stork" Hendricks

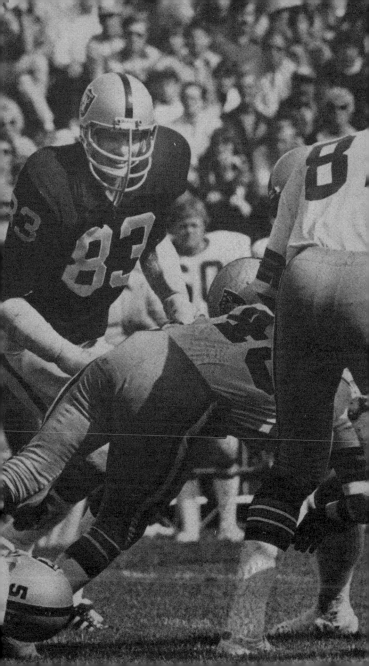

the game," said Jaworski afterward. "Emotion is important for us. Intensity and emotion they never seemed to develop. If I knew why, I'd be teaching psychology at some university."

The Eagles never recovered from their early 14–0 deficit. They got only a field goal of 30 yards by Tony Franklin, the barefoot kicker who had been in a slump in recent weeks. But another attempt of his was blocked by Ted ("The Stork") Hendricks, the 6-8 middle and roving linebacker.

The Eagles didn't score their touchdowns until the final period, but by then the game had been set on its course. Plunkett was mixing the long pass with his running game, passing to Mark van Eeghen and Kenny King. Van Eeghen, who is from Colgate, carried 19 times for 80 yards.

King, who had been cut by the Oilers, made the most sensational play of the game on the second touchdown. "I'm not in the shadows of anyone anymore," he said, alluding to Earl Campbell. "I have my own mold and my own team."

Oakland's third touchdown came on a pass reception by Branch, for his second of two TD catches. It came in the third quarter, and he and rookie cornerback Roynell Young wrestled for Plunkett's 29-yard pass into the end zone, with Branch's half-nelson succeeding. That gave the Raiders a 21–3 lead, which Bahr shortly after increased to 24–3 on a 46-yard field goal.

Starting the fourth quarter, Jaworski connected with Keith Krepfle on an 8-yard score. He caught the ball and quickly looked down, thinking he might be out of the end zone (a salient comment on the uncertainty with which the Eagles played this game—even when they were doing something positive).

Then Bahr split the uprights and pushed the Raider margin to 27–10 with 8:29 to play.

The Eagles still had a chance, however, no matter how remote it seemed. They needed two touchdowns and a field goal in less than seven minutes in order to tie. Well, stranger things have happened in pro football. The unexpected has come to be, if not wholly expected, then at least anticipated.

Jaworski was now starting to get a drive together. But on the fifth play, with about five and a half minutes remaining, he fumbled the snap and the Raiders recovered. On his next possession Jaworski threw his third interception, sealing the Eagles' fate.

When the final whistle blew, it heralded not just the end of the game but perhaps the most dramatic moment of the day—the awarding of the Super Bowl trophy by Pete Rozelle, commissioner of the NFL, to Al Davis, managing partner (or major owner) of the Raiders. Rozelle and Davis do not get along. In fact, before the Super Bowl, Davis filed suit against the NFL because Rózelle had blocked Davis's proposed move to Los Angeles (where he said the stadium seating capacity would greatly increase his team's revenues). Rozelle contended that the Raiders have a good franchise right where they are—in Oakland.

And so when the cheering stopped and the 75,500 fans started to leave the Louisiana Superdome, Davis and Rozelle had their own confrontation.

When Rozelle presented the trophy to Davis in the dressing room and Davis mumbled, "Thanks very much, thanks very much, Commissioner," they were surrounded by innumerable cameras that had sprung up like weeds. "It looked like a Japanese bus tour as the Raider players themselves hoisted their cameras in the air to capture the moment forever," wrote Paul Zimmerman in *Sports Illustrated*.

But there was no clash between the pair on the stand, and it was all cordiality—on the surface. Rozelle went on to praise Davis for the work he and his organization had done with this team. Not a word was said about their problems.

Then Davis went over to Gene Upshaw, the senior veteran on the Raiders (he has been with them since he was a first-round draft pick in 1967). Upshaw, at 35 years of age, had talked about retiring after this season.

"What do you say, are you going to let me retire now?" asked Upshaw.

"It's up to you," said Davis.

"Ah heck, I can't retire. I've got minicamp coming up in March."

The Raiders, it seems, aren't finished yet.

Super Bowl Summary

Raiders-Eagles Scoring

Oak.	Phil.	FIRST QUARTER
7	0	Branch, 2, pass from Plunkett (Bahr, kick) at 6 minutes 4 seconds. 30 yards in 7 plays after Martin intercepts pass by Jaworski on Eagle 46 and returns 16 yards. Key play: Branch, 14, pass from Plunkett.
14	0	King, 80, pass from Plunkett (Bahr, kick) at 14:51.86 yards in 3 plays.

Oak.	Phil.	

SECOND QUARTER

| 14 | 3 | Franklin, FG, 30, at 4:32. 61 yards in 9 plays. Key plays: Montgomery, 8, run; Spagnola, 22, and Montgomery, 25, passes from Jaworski. |

THIRD QUARTER

| 21 | 3 | Branch, 29, pass from Plunkett (Bahr, kick) at 2:36. 76 yards in 5 plays. Key plays: Chandler, 32, pass from Plunkett. |
| 24 | 3 | Bahr, FG, 46, at 10:25. 40 yards in 8 plays after Martin intercepts pass by Jaworski and returns 2 yards to Raider 32. Key plays: Chester, 16 and 17, passes from Plunkett. |

FOURTH QUARTER

| 24 | 10 | Krepfle, 8, pass from Jaworski (Franklin, kick) at 1:01. 88 yards in 12 plays. Key plays: Smith, 43, pass from Jaworski; Parker, 19, pass from Jaworski on fourth-and-7. |
| 27 | 10 | Bahr, FG, 35, at 6:31. 72 yards in 12 plays. Key plays: van Eeghen, 8, run; Chandler, 23, pass from Plunkett. |

Super Bowl Statistics

Oakland .... 14 0 10 3—27
Philadelphia ..... 0 3 0 7—10

INDIVIDUAL LEADERS

RUSHING—Oakland, van Eeghen 19-80, King 6-18, Jensen 3-12, Plunkett 3-9, Whittington 3-minus 2. Philadelphia, Montgomery 16-44, Harris 7-14, Giammona 1-7, Harrington 1-4, Jaworski 1-0.

PASSING—Oakland, Plunkett 13-21-0-261. Philadelphia, Jaworski 18-38-3-291.

RECEIVING—Oakland, Branch 5-67, Chandler 4-77, King 2-93, Chester 2-24. Philadelphia, Montgomery 6-91, Carmichael 5-83, Smith 2-59, Krepfle 2-16, Spagnola 1-22, Parker 1-19, Harris 1-1.

INTERCEPTIONS—Oakland, Martin 3-44.

KICKOFF RETURNS—Oakland, Matthews 2-29, Moody 1-19. Philadelphia, Campfield 5-87.

A—75,500

	Oak.	Phi.
First downs	17	19
Rushes-yards	34-117	26-69
Passing yards	260	291
Return yards	45	20
Passes	13-21-0	18-38-3
Punts	3-42	3-37
Fumbles-lost	0-0	1-1
Penalties-yards	5-37	6-57
Field goals	2-3	1-2
Time of possession..	29:49	30:11

Super Bowl Records

Records Set

Most Interceptions—3, Rod Martin, Oakland.
Longest Pass Play—80 yards, Jim Plunkett to Kenny King, Oakland.
Most Passes—38, Ron Jaworski, Philadelphia.
Most Yards Gained Passing, Both Teams—551: Philadelphia (291), Oakland (260).
Fewest Times Tackled Attempting to Pass, Both Teams—1: Philadelphia (0), Oakland (1).
Fewest Punts, Both Teams—6: Oakland (3), Philadelphia (3).

Records Tied

Most Touchdowns by Player—2, Cliff Branch, Oakland.
Most Touchdown Passes Caught—2, Branch.
Most Completions—18, Jaworski.
Most Interceptions, Career—3, Martin.
Most Kickoff Returns—5, Billy Campfield, Philadelphia.
Most Points, First Quarter, Team—14, Oakland.
Most Points, First Quarter, Both Teams—14: Oakland (14), Philadelphia (0).
Fewest Touchdowns, Rushing, Both Teams—0.
Fewest Times Tackled, Attempting To Pass, Team—0, Philadelphia.
Fewest Fumbles, Team—0, Oakland.

Pro Bowl
NFC 21, AFC 7
Aloha Stadium, Honolulu
Sunday, February 1, 1981

EDDIE MURRAY, SLIGHT FOR A pro football player at 5'10", 170 pounds, and rather meek looking with a boyish haircut parted down the middle, stood on the Aloha Stadium turf before the Pro Bowl game—the All-Star game between the NFC and the AFC—and couldn't believe that a year ago he wasn't even sure he was good enough to play professional football. Now he was a member of the NFC team, one of five rookies (out of 80 players), along with his better-known rookie teammate on the Detroit Lions, Billy Sims.

Not only had he become a professional. Not only had he become an all-star in his rookie season. But now he was the star of the game, leading the NFC to a 21–7 win by kicking four field goals.

The year before, the soccer-style kicker who was born in Halifax, Nova Scotia, was setting school records for kicking at Tulane.

"Last year I watched this game [Pro Bowl] on television," Murray said after the game. "At that time I didn't even know whether I'd make it in the league, much less this game.

"I can't believe it. The Pro Bowl has definitely been the highlight of my rookie year."

Murray was named the Most Valuable Player as he helped the NFC gain a 7–5 advantage in the Pro Bowl series. He missed tying Garo Yepremian's seven-year-old record of five field goals in a Pro Bowl when a 37-yard attempt hit the cross bar with 22 seconds left. He also missed a 37-yarder in the first quarter.

But it was some season for him, as he led the NFC in scoring for the regular season, totaling 116 points on 35 for 36 extra points and 27 out of 42 field goals. His 27 field goals made were the highest of any kicker in pro ball.

Murray led off the scoring in the Pro Bowl with a 31-yard field goal in the first quarter, the only score in that period.

Steve Bartkowski, the quarterback, and Alfred Jenkins, Bartkowski's teammate from the Atlanta Falcons, combined on a 55-yard scoring pass for the NFC's only touchdown.

"The touchdown play was called as an option screen, but I gave Steve our signal when I saw the cornerback come up," Jenkins said.

Bartkowski was almost apologetic about the lack of offense, saying, "We're limited to just three pass patterns, and we really just didn't have time to get everything cohesive."

The NFC displayed an excellent defense, however, led by Lee Roy Selmon, the Tampa Bay linebacker, and Randy White, the Dallas tackle. "Our secondary did a great job and gave the defensive line time to get the quarterback," Selmon said.

Rookie Sensation Billy Sims

After the NFC had taken a 9–7 halftime lead—on two more kicks by Murray, of 31 and 34 yards—Bartkowski hit Jenkins in the fourth quarter. Murray then added his fourth field goal, from the 36.

Both the touchdown and the final field goal were set up when Jack Reynolds, the Los Angeles linebacker, stopped Joe Cribbs of Buffalo on fourth-and-1 plays.

The AFC's only score came on a 9-yard pass from Brian Sipe of Cleveland to Stanley Morgan of New England in the second quarter.

The play was relatively sloppy. The AFC was penalized nine times for 74 yards and the NFC 10 times for 60 yards. There were three fumbles lost and four interceptions before a crowd of 50,360 in Aloha Stadium.

The selections for the team were made by all the coaches, with some input by players during the last week of the regular season. Coaches and players had to vote for those in their conference and could not choose teammates.

"Being with the best football players in the world is a kick for me," said Cleveland's Sam Rutigliano, coach of the AFC.

His opposite number was Leeman Bennett of Atlanta. "I just hope that I don't mess them up so much that they don't win."

The AFC didn't win. But no one blamed Rutigliano. It was a case of too much of one rookie, Eddie Murray. Last year he had watched the game on TV. This year he had the best seat in the house: the hero's pedestal.

Pro Bowl star Steve Bartkowski of the Atlanta Falcons was a leader in touchdown passes.

III
1980
STATISTICS

INDIVIDUAL 1980 STATISTICS

NFC
Leading Scorers

Touchdowns

	TDs	Rush	Rec	Ret	Pts
Sims, Det.	16	13	3	0	96
Dorsett, Dall.	11	11	0	0	66
Brown, Minn.	10	8	2	0	60
Gray, N.Y.	10	0	10	0	60
Montgomery, Phil. ...	10	8	2	0	60
Solomon, S.F.	10	0	8	2	60
Anderson, St.L.	9	9	0	0	54
Cain, Atl.	9	8	1	0	54
Carmichael, Phil.	9	0	9	0	54
Cooper, S.F.	9	5	4	0	54
J. Miller, Atl.	9	0	9	0	54
Peacock, L.A.	9	7	2	0	54

Kicking

	PAT	FG	LG	Pts
Murray, Det.	35/36	27/42	52	116
Mazzetti, Atl.	46/49	19/27	50	103
Corral, L.A.	51/52	16/30	47	99
Franklin, Phil.	48/48	16/31	51	96
Septien, Dall.	59/60	11/17	52	92
Danmeier, Minn.	33/38	16/26	47	81
Moseley, Wash.	27/30	18/33	52	81
Yepremian, T.B.	31/32	16/23	43	79
Wersching, S.F.	33/39	15/19	47	78
Danelo, N.Y.	27/27	16/24	51	75
Thomas, Chi.	35/37	13/18	44	74
Ricardo, N.O.	31/34	10/17	47	61

Best Performance: 24 pts.; Gray, N.Y. *vs.* St.L. 9/7 (4 TDs)
Longest Field Goal: 52 yds., Murray, Det. *vs.* L.A. 9/7
52 yds., Moseley, Wash. *vs.* N.O. 10/26
52 yds., Septien, Dall. *vs.* Oak. 12/7

INDIVIDUAL 1980 STATISTICS

AFC
Leading Scorers

Touchdowns

	TDs	Rush	Rec	Ret	Pts
Campbell, Hou.	13	13	0	0	78
Dickey, Balt.	13	11	2	0	78
Jefferson, S.D.	13	0	13	0	78
Cribbs, Buff.	12	11	1	0	72
Chandler, Oak.	10	0	10	0	60
Calhoun, N.E.	9	9	0	0	54
Smith, Pitt.	9	0	9	0	54
Winslow, S.D.	9	0	9	0	54
Francis, N.E.	8	0	8	0	48

Kicking

	PAT	FG	LG	Pts
Smith, N.E.	51/51	26/34	44	129
Benirschke, S.D.	46/48	24/36	53	118
Steinfort, Den.	32/33	26/34	57	110
Bahr, Oak.	41/44	19/37	48	98
Lowery, K.C.	37/37	20/26	57	97
Bahr, Pitt.	39/42	19/28	48	96
Herrera, Sea.	33/33	20/31	50	93
Cockroft, Clev.	39/44	16/26	45	87
Fritsch, Hou.	26/27	19/24	46	83

Best Performance: 18 pts., Smith, Pitt. *vs.* Chi. 9/28 (3 TDs)
18 pts., Chandler, Oak. *vs.* Sea. 10/26 (3 TDs)
Longest Field Goal: 57 yds., Lowery, K.C. *vs.* Sea. 9/14
57 yds., Steinfort, Den. *vs.* Wash. 10/13

NFC
Leading Rushers

	Att	Yards	Avg	Long	TDs
Payton, Chi.	317	1460	4.6	69	6
Anderson, St.L.	301	1352	4.5	52	9
Andrews, Atl.	265	1308	4.9	33	4
Sims, Det.	313	1303	4.2	52	13
Dorsett, Dall.	278	1185	4.3	56	11
Cain, Atl.	235	914	3.9	37	8
Brown, Minn.	219	912	4.2	55	8
Ivery, G.B.	202	831	4.1	38	3
Bryant, L.A.	183	807	4.4	20	3
Montgomery, Phil.	193	778	4.0	72	8
Peacock, L.A.	164	777	4.7	36	7
Bussey, Det.	145	720	5.0	40	3
Cooper, S.F.	171	720	4.2	47	5
Jackson, Wash.	176	708	4.0	55	3
Bell, T.B.	174	599	3.4	40	2
Taylor, N.Y.	147	580	3.9	35	4
Ellis, G.B.	126	545	4.3	22	5
Eckwood, T.B.	149	504	3.4	35	2
Harmon, Wash.	128	484	3.8	23	4
Morris, St.L.	117	456	3.9	24	6

Best Performance: 183 yds. (18 attempts), Payton, Chi. *vs.* N.O. 9/14—1 TD
183 yds. (24 attempts), Dorsett, Dall. *vs.* N.Y.G. 11/9—2 TDs
Longest: 72 yds., Montgomery, Phil. *vs.* Minn. 9/14—TD

AFC
Leading Rushers

	Att	Yards	Avg	Long	TDs
Campbell, Hou.	373	1934	5.2	55	13
Cribbs, Buff.	306	1185	3.9	48	11
M. Pruitt, Clev.	249	1034	4.2	56	6
van Eeghen, Oak.	222	838	3.8	34	5
Muncie, S.D.	175	827	4.7	53	6
Ferguson, N.E.	211	818	3.9	44	2
Dickey, Balt.	176	800	4.5	51	11
Harris, Pitt.	208	789	3.8	26	4
Calhoun, N.E.	200	787	3.9	22	9
King, Oak.	172	761	4.4	89	4
Johnson, Cin.	186	747	4.0	57	6
Alexander, Cin.	169	702	4.2	37	2
McKnight, K.C.	206	693	3.4	25	3
Williams, Mia.	187	671	3.6	65	2
Jodat, Sea.	155	632	4.1	26	5
Dierking, N.Y.	156	567	3.6	15	6
Brown, Buff.	153	559	3.7	34	3
Washington, Balt.	144	502	3.5	17	1
Thomas, S.D.	118	484	4.1	18	3
Jensen, Den.	101	476	4.7	32	2

Best Performance: 206 yds. (31 attempts), Campbell, Hou. *vs.* Chi. 11/16
Longest: 89 yds., King, Oak. *vs.* S.D. 10/12—TD

N F C
Leading Passers
(192 attempts)

	Att	Comp	Pct Comp	Yds Gnd	Avg Yds Gained	TD Pass	Pct TD	Long	Int	Pct Int	Rating
Jaworski, Phil.	451	257	57.0	3529	7.82	27	6.0	56	12	2.7	90.9
Ferragamo, L.A.	404	240	59.4	3199	7.92	30	7.4	74	19	4.7	89.7
Bartkowski, Atl.	463	257	55.5	3544	7.65	31	6.7	81	16	3.5	88.0
Montana, S.F.	273	176	64.5	1795	6.58	15	5.5	71	9	3.3	87.8
Danielson, Det.	417	244	58.5	3223	7.73	13	3.1	87	11	2.6	82.6
Manning, N.O.	509	309	60.7	3716	7.30	23	4.5	56	20	3.9	81.8
D. White, Dall.	436	260	59.6	3287	7.54	28	6.4	58	25	5.7	80.8
Theismann, Wash.	454	262	57.7	2962	6.52	17	3.7	54	16	3.5	75.1
Kramer, Minn.	522	299	57.3	3582	6.86	19	3.6	76	23	4.4	72.1
Dickey, G.B.	478	278	58.2	3529	7.38	15	3.1	69	25	5.2	70.0
Williams, T.B.	521	254	48.8	3396	6.52	20	3.8	61	16	3.1	69.7
Hart, St.L.	425	228	53.6	2946	6.93	16	3.8	69	20	4.7	68.7
DeBerg, S.F.	321	186	57.9	1998	6.22	12	3.7	93	17	5.3	66.5
Evans, Chi.	278	148	53.2	2039	7.33	11	4.0	89	16	5.8	66.1
Simms, N.Y.	402	193	48.0	2321	5.77	15	3.7	58	19	4.7	58.9

Longest: 93 yds., DeBerg (to Solomon), S.F. vs Atl. 9/28—TD

AFC
Leading Passers
(192 attempts)

	Att	Comp	Pct Comp	Yds Gnd	Avg Yds Gained	TD Pass	Pct TD	Long	Int	Pct Int	Rating
Sipe, Clev.	554	340	61.4	4132	7.46	30	5.4	65	14	2.5	91.9
Fouts, S.D.	589	348	59.1	4715	8.01	30	5.1	65	24	4.1	84.6
Morton, Den.	301	183	60.8	2150	7.14	12	4.0	41	13	4.3	77.9
Fuller, K.C.	320	193	60.3	2250	7.03	10	3.1	77	12	3.8	76.1
B. Jones, Balt.	446	248	55.6	3134	7.03	23	5.2	47	21	4.7	75.5
Bradshaw, Pitt.	424	218	51.4	3339	7.88	24	5.7	68	22	5.2	75.1
Ferguson, Buff.	439	251	57.2	2805	6.39	20	46	69	18	4.1	74.6
Grogan, N.E.	306	175	57.2	2475	8.09	18	5.9	71	22	7.2	73.1
Plunkett, Oak.	320	165	51.6	2299	7.18	18	5.6	86	16	5.0	72.8
Zorn, Sea.	488	276	56.6	3346	6.86	17	3.5	67	20	4.1	72.4
Stabler, Hou.	457	293	64.1	3202	7.01	13	2.8	79	28	6.1	68.6
Anderson, Cinn.	275	166	60.4	1778	6.47	6	2.2	67	13	4.7	67.1
Woodley, Mia.	327	176	53.8	1850	5.66	14	4.3	61	17	5.2	63.2
Todd, N.Y.	479	264	55.1	3329	6.95	17	3.5	55	30	6.3	62.4
Thompson, Cin.	234	115	49.1	1324	5.66	11	4.7	59	12	5.1	61.0

Longest: 86 yds., Plunkett (to Branch), Oak. vs. Phil. 11/23—TD

NFC
Leading Pass Receivers

Receptions

	No	Yards	Avg	TDs
Cooper, S.F. (rb)	83	567	6.8	4
Clark, S.F.	82	991	12.1	8
Lofton, G.B.	71	1226	17.3	4
Rashad, Minn.	69	1095	15.9	5
Tilley, St.L.	68	966	14.2	6
Chandler, N.O.	65	975	15.0	6
Young, Minn. (rb)	64	499	7.8	2
Brown, Minn. (rb)	62	623	10.0	2
Hill, Dall.	60	1055	17.6	8
Monk, Wash.	58	797	13.7	3
Jenkins, Atl.	57	1026	18.0	6
Galbreath, N.O. (rb)	57	470	8.2	2
Francis, Atl.	54	862	16.0	7
Harmon, Wash. (rb)	54	534	9.9	4
S. White, Minn.	53	887	16.7	5
Scott, Det.	53	834	15.7	4
Bryant, L.A. (rb)	53	386	7.3	3
Gray, N.Y.	52	777	14.9	10
Sims, Det. (rb)	51	621	12.2	3
Andrews, Atl. (rb)	51	456	8.9	1

*The NFC Leader in Yards Gained by a
Receiver, Lofton of Green Bay*

Yards

	Yards	No	Avg	TDs
Lofton, G.B.	1226	71	17.3	4
Rashad, Minn.	1095	69	15.9	5
Hill, Dall.	1055	60	17.6	8
Jenkins, Atl.	1026	57	18.0	6
Clark, S.F.	991	82	12.1	8
Chandler, N.O.	975	65	15.0	6
Tilley, St.L.	966	68	14.2	6
S. White, Minn.	887	53	16.7	5
Francis, Atl.	862	54	16.0	7
Scott, Det.	834	53	15.7	4
Smith, Phil.	825	47	17.6	3
Carmichael, Phil.	815	48	17.0	9
Monk, Wash.	797	58	13.7	3
Gray, N.Y.	777	52	14.9	10
Gray, St.L.	709	40	17.7	3
Scott, Chi.	696	36	19.3	3
Harris, N.O.	692	37	18.7	6
Waddy, L.A.	670	38	17.6	5
Jones, T.B.	669	48	13.9	5
Solomon, S.F.	658	48	13.7	8

Most Receptions: 12 (118 yds.), Harmon, Wash. *vs.* S.D. 12/7
Most Yards: 175 (8 receptions), Lofton, G. B. *vs.* N.Y.G. 11/16—1
TD

AFC
Leading Pass Receivers

Receptions

	No	Yards	Avg	TDs
Winslow, S.D.	89	1290	14.5	9
Jefferson, S.D.	82	1340	16.3	13
Joiner, S.D.	71	1132	15.9	4
Largent, Sea.	66	1064	16.1	6
M. Pruitt, Clev. (rb)	63	471	7.5	0
McCullum, Sea.	62	874	14.1	6
Carr, Balt.	61	924	15.1	5
Barber, Hou.	59	712	12.1	5
Butler, Buff.	57	832	14.6	6
Nathan, Mia. (rb)	57	588	10.3	5
Casper, Hou.	56	796	14.2	4
Ross, Cin.	56	724	12.9	4
Rucker, Clev.	55	768	14.0	4
Cribbs, Buff. (rb)	52	415	3.0	1
Logan, Clev.	51	822	16.1	4
Newsome, Clev.	51	594	11.6	3
Washington, Balt. (rb)	51	494	9.7	3
Harper, N.Y. (rb)	50	634	12.7	3
G. Pruitt, Clev. (rb)	50	444	8.9	5
Chandler, Oak.	49	786	16.0	10
Jensen, Den. (rb)	49	377	7.7	1

Yards

	Yards	No	Avg	TDs
Jefferson, S.D.	1340	82	16.3	13
Winslow, S.D.	1290	89	14.5	9
Joiner, S.D.	1132	71	15.9	4
Largent, Sea.	1064	66	16.1	6
Morgan, N.E.	991	45	22.0	6
Carr, Balt.	924	61	15.1	5
McCullum, Sea.	874	62	14.1	6
Branch, Oak.	858	44	19.5	7
Butler, Buff.	832	57	14.6	6
Logan, Clev.	822	51	16.1	4
Marshall, K.C.	799	47	17.0	6
Casper, Hou.	796	56	14.2	4
Chandler, Oak.	786	49	16.0	10
Rucker, Clev.	768	55	14.0	4
Bell, Pitt.	748	29	25.8	2
Jackson, N.E.	737	35	21.1	5
Ross, Cin.	724	56	12.9	4
Barber, Hou.	712	59	12.1	5
Smith, Pitt.	711	37	19.2	9
Swann, Pitt.	710	44	16.1	7
Moses, Den.	674	38	17.7	4

Most Receptions: 17 (160 yds.), Gaines, N.Y. *vs.* S.F. 9/21
Most Yards: 176 (7 receptions), Curtis, Cin. *vs.* Balt. 12/7
176 (9 receptions), Marshall, K.C. *vs.* Balt. 12/21

NFC
Leading Punters

	No	Yds	Long	Avg	TB	Blk	Ret	Ret Yds	In 20	Net Avg
Jennings, N.Y.	94	4211	63	44.8	13	0	58	506	16	36.6
Blanchard, T.B.	88	3722	62	42.3	12	1	54	529	18	33.2
Skladany, Det.	72	3036	67	42.2	8	1	38	300	16	35.3
Swider, St.L.	99	4111	66	41.5	15	1	62	645	12	31.7
Miller, S.F.	77	3152	65	40.9	5	0	48	530	11	32.8
D. White, Dall.	71	2903	58	40.9	11	0	32	215	17	34.8
Parsons, Chi.	79	3207	61	40.6	10	0	46	415	16	32.8
Corral, L.A.	76	3002	65	39.5	5	1	42	353	14	33.1
Erxleben, N.O.	89	3499	57	39.3	3	0	48	490	23	33.1
Runager, Phil.	75	2947	58	39.3	8	1	35	224	16	33.7
Connell, Wash.	85	3331	57	39.2	7	0	52	351	11	33.4
James, Atl.	79	3087	59	39.1	7	0	36	240	25	34.3
Coleman, Minn.	81	3139	65	38.8	8	0	42	259	20	33.6
Beverly, G.B.	86	3294	55	38.3	6	0	50	342	18	32.9

Longest: 67 yds., Skladany, Det. *vs.* Minn. 11/9

AFC
Leading Punters

	No	Yds	Long	Avg	TB	Blk	Ret	Ret Yds	In 20	Net Avg
Prestridge, Den.	70	3075	57	43.9	6	0	52	443	10	35.9
Guy, Oak.	71	3099	66	43.6	14	0	34	268	18	35.9
Roberts, Mia.	77	3279	71	42.6	8	2	42	339	18	35.2
Ramsey, N.Y.	73	3096	59	42.4	10	1	46	369	15	34.1
Weaver, Sea.	67	2798	62	41.8	7	2	42	476	14	31.6
McInally, Cin.	83	3390	61	40.8	13	2	45	476	21	31.2
Colquitt, Pitt.	61	2483	54	40.7	5	0	34	217	13	35.5
Parsley, Hou.	67	2727	57	40.7	8	0	40	394	19	32.4
Grupp, K.C.	84	3317	57	39.5	8	1	44	289	23	33.7
Partridge, S.D.	60	2347	55	39.1	3	1	43	359	10	31.6
Cater, Buff.	73	2828	61	38.7	16	1	34	204	12	31.1
Bragg, Balt.	83	3199	59	38.5	6	1	50	357	22	32.4
Evans, Clev.	66	2530	56	38.3	7	0	38	245	12	32.5
Hubach, N.E.	63	2392	69	38.0	2	0	28	237	12	33.6

Longest: 71 yds., Roberts, Mia. vs. Oak. 11/2

NFC
Punt Return Leaders

	No	Yards	Avg	Long	TDs
Johnson, Atl.	23	281	12.2	56	0
Solomon, S.F.	27	298	11.0	57	2
Green, St.L.	16	168	10.5	57	1
J. Jones, Dall.	54	548	10.1	52	0
Nelms, Wash.	48	487	10.1	64	0
R. Smith, Atl.	27	262	9.7	25	0
R. Williams, Det.	27	259	9.6	53	0
Bell, St.L.	21	195	9.3	54	0
Sciarra, Phil.	36	330	9.2	32	0
Henry, Phil.	26	222	8.5	30	0
Garrett, N.Y.	35	287	8.2	66	0
Cassidy, G.B.	17	139	8.2	20	0
Payton, Minn.	34	251	7.4	19	0
Arnold, Det.	28	204	7.3	19	0

Longest: 66 yds., Garrett, N.Y. *vs.* St.L. 9/7

AFC
Punt Return Leaders

	No	Yards	Avg	Long	TDs
J.T. Smith, K.C.	40	581	14.5	75	2
James, N.E.	33	331	10.0	75	1
Bell, Pitt.	34	339	10.0	27	0
Fuller, S.D.	30	298	9.9	31	0
Upchurch, Den.	37	353	9.5	34	0
Matthews, Oak.	48	421	8.8	34	0
Harper, N.Y.	28	242	8.6	24	0
Lewis, Sea.	41	349	8.5	75	1
Haynes, N.E.	17	140	8.2	35	0
Roaches, Hou.	47	384	8.2	68	0
Glasgow, Balt.	23	187	8.1	20	0
Nathan, Mia.	23	178	7.7	30	0
Montgomery, Cin.	31	223	7.2	42	0

Longest: 75 yds., James, N.E. *vs.* N.Y.J. 11/2—TD
75 yds., Lewis, Sea. *vs.* Den. 11/23—TD
75 yds., Smith, K.C. *vs.* St.L. 11/23—TD

NFC
Kickoff Return Leaders

	No	Yards	Avg	Long	TDs
Mauti, N.O.	31	798	25.7	52	0
Williams, Chi.	27	666	24.7	95	1
Owens, S.F.	31	726	23.4	101	1
Green, St.L.	32	745	23.3	37	0
Rogers, N.O.	41	930	22.7	88	0
J. Jones, Dall.	32	720	22.5	41	0
Payton, Minn.	53	1184	22.3	59	0
G. Davis, T.B.	44	951	21.6	54	0
Kane, Det.	23	495	21.5	62	0
Suhey, Chi.	19	406	21.4	31	0
Nelms, Wash.	38	810	21.3	51	0
Campfield, Phil.	26	540	20.8	33	0
R. Smith, Atl.	25	512	20.5	35	0
D. Hill, L.A.	43	880	20.5	98	1

Longest: 101 yds., Owens, S.F. *vs.* Det. 11/2—TD

AFC
Kickoff Return Leaders

	No	Yards	Avg	Long	TDs
Ivory, N.E.	36	992	27.6	98	1
Lewis, Sea.	25	585	23.4	54	0
Brunson, Den.	40	923	23.1	53	0
Wright, Clev.	25	576	23.0	50	0
Carson, K.C.	40	917	22.9	47	0
Glasgow, Balt.	33	743	22.5	44	0
Pollard, Pitt.	22	494	22.5	34	0
Bessillieu, Mia.	40	890	22.3	87	0
Harper, N.Y.	49	1070	21.8	35	0
D. Hall, Clev.	32	691	21.6	40	0
Muncie, S.D.	16	344	21.5	44	0
Matthews, Oak.	29	585	20.2	45	0
Roaches, Hou.	37	746	20.2	46	0

Longest: 98 yds., Ivory, N.E. *vs.* Balt. 10/19—TD

NFC
Interception Leaders

	No	Yards	Long	TDs
Cromwell, L.A.	8	140	34	1
Richardson, Atl.	7	139	52	0
Parrish, Wash.	7	13	9	0
Lavender, Wash.	6	96	51	1
Wilson, Phil.	6	79	41	0
Murphy, Wash.	6	58	28	0
Allen, Det.	6	38	23	0
Turner, Minn.	6	22	13	0
Hunter, Det.	6	20	13	0

Longest: 99 yds., Johnson, L.A. *vs.* G.B. 9/21—TD

AFC
Interception Leaders

	No	Yards	Long	TDs
Hayes, Oak.	13	273	62	1
Barbaro, K.C.	10	163	39	0
Schroy, N.Y.	8	91	82	1
Shell, Pitt.	7	135	67	0
Freeman, Buff.	7	107	47	1
Tatum, Hou.	7	100	35	0
Breeden, Cin.	7	91	29	0
Harris, K.C.	7	54	41	0
Small, Mia.	7	46	22	0

Longest: 93 yds., Gradishar, Den. *vs.* Clev. 10/5—TD

STANDINGS AND CLUB RECORDS

NFC
1980 Final Standings

Eastern Division

		W	L	T	Pct	Pts	OP
*	Philadelphia	12	4	0	.750	384	222
#	Dallas	12	4	0	.750	454	311
	Washington	6	10	0	.375	261	293
	St. Louis	5	11	0	.313	299	350
	N.Y. Giants	4	12	0	.250	249	425

Central Division

		W	L	T	Pct	Pts	OP
*	Minnesota	9	7	0	.563	317	308
	Detroit	9	7	0	.563	334	272
	Chicago	7	9	0	.438	304	264
	Tampa Bay	5	10	1	.344	271	341
	Green Bay	5	10	1	.344	231	371

Western Division

		W	L	T	Pct	Pts	OP
*	Atlanta	12	4	0	.750	405	272
#	Los Angeles	11	5	0	.688	424	289
	San Francisco	6	10	0	.375	320	415
	New Orleans	1	15	0	.063	291	487

*Division Champion
#Wild Card for Play-Offs

STANDINGS AND CLUB RECORDS

AFC
1980 Final Standings

Eastern Division

		W	L	T	Pct	Pts	OP
*	Buffalo	11	5	0	.688	320	260
	New England	10	6	0	.625	441	325
	Miami	8	8	0	.500	266	305
	Baltimore	7	9	0	.438	355	387
	N.Y. Jets	4	12	0	.250	302	395

Central Division

		W	L	T	Pct	Pts	OP
*	Cleveland	11	5	0	.688	357	310
#	Houston	11	5	0	.688	295	251
	Pittsburgh	9	7	0	.563	352	313
	Cincinnati	6	10	0	.375	244	312

Western Division

		W	L	T	Pct	Pts	OP
*	San Diego	11	5	0	.688	418	327
#	Oakland	11	5	0	.688	364	306
	Kansas City	8	8	0	.500	319	336
	Denver	8	8	0	.500	310	323
	Seattle	4	12	0	.250	291	408

*Division Champion
#Wild Card for Play-Offs

CLUB-BY-CLUB 1980 STANDINGS

NFC
Eastern Division

Philadelphia Eagles (12–4)

27	DENVER	6
42	at Minnesota	7
35	NEW YORK GIANTS	3*
14	at St. Louis	24*
24	WASHINGTON	14*
31	at New York Giants	16*
17	DALLAS	10*
17	CHICAGO	14
27	at Seattle	20
34	at New Orleans	21
24	at Washington	0*
10	OAKLAND	7
21	at San Diego	22
17	ATLANTA	20
17	ST. LOUIS	3*
27	at Dallas	35*
384		**222**

Dallas Cowboys (12–4)

17	at Washington	3*
20	at Denver	41
28	TAMPA BAY	17
28	at Green Bay	7
24	NEW YORK GIANTS	3*
59	SAN FRANCISCO	14
10	at Philadelphia	17*
42	SAN DIEGO	31
27	at St. Louis	24*
35	at New York Giants	38*
31	ST. LOUIS	21*
14	WASHINGTON	10*
51	SEATTLE	7
19	at Oakland	13
14	at Los Angeles	38
35	PHILADELPHIA	27*
454		**311**

*Intradivisional Games

Washington Redskins (6–10)

3	DALLAS	17*
23	at New York Giants	21*
21	at Oakland	24
0	SEATTLE	14
14	at Philadelphia	24*
17	at Denver	20
23	ST. LOUIS	0*
22	NEW ORLEANS	14
14	MINNESOTA	39
21	at Chicago	35
0	PHILADELPHIA	24*
10	at Dallas	14*
6	at Atlanta	10
40	SAN DIEGO	17
16	NEW YORK GIANTS	13*
31	at St. Louis	7*
261		293

St. Louis Cardinals (5–11)

35	NEW YORK GIANTS	41*
21	at San Francisco	24 (OT)
7	at Detroit	20
24	PHILADELPHIA	14*
40	at New Orleans	7
13	LOS ANGELES	21
0	at Washington	23*
17	at Baltimore	10
24	DALLAS	27*
27	ATLANTA	33 (OT)
21	at Dallas	31*
13	KANSAS CITY	21
23	at New York Giants	7*
24	DETROIT	23
3	at Philadelphia	17*
7	WASHINGTON	31*
299		350

*Intradivisional Games

New York Giants (4–12)

41	at St. Louis	35*
21	WASHINGTON	23*
3	at Philadelphia	35*
7	LOS ANGELES	28
3	at Dallas	24*
16	PHILADELPHIA	31*
7	at San Diego	44
9	DENVER	14
13	at Tampa Bay	30
38	DALLAS	35*
27	GREEN BAY	21
0	at San Francisco	12
7	ST. LOUIS	23*
27	at Seattle	21
13	at Washington	16*
17	OAKLAND	33
249		425

Central Division

Minnesota Vikings (9–7)

24	ATLANTA	23
7	PHILADELPHIA	42
34	at Chicago	14*
7	at Detroit	27*
17	PITTSBURGH	23
13	CHICAGO	7*
0	at Cincinnati	14
3	at Green Bay	16*
39	at Washington	14
34	DETROIT	0*
38	TAMPA BAY	30*
13	GREEN BAY	25*
23	at New Orleans	20
21	at Tampa Bay	10*
28	CLEVELAND	23
16	at Houston	20
317		308

*Intradivisional Games

Detroit Lions (9–7)

41	at Los Angeles	20
29	at Green Bay	7*
20	ST. LOUIS	7
27	MINNESOTA	7*
28	at Atlanta	43
24	NEW ORLEANS	13
7	at Chicago	24*
17	at Kansas City	20
17	SAN FRANCISCO	13
0	at Minnesota	34*
9	BALTIMORE	10
24	at Tampa Bay	10*
17	CHICAGO	23 (OT)*
23	at St. Louis	24
27	TAMPA BAY	14*
24	GREEN BAY	3*
334		272

Chicago Bears (7–9)

6	at Green Bay	12 (OT)*
22	NEW ORLEANS	3
14	MINNESOTA	34*
3	at Pittsburgh	38
23	TAMPA BAY	0*
7	at Minnesota	13*
24	DETROIT	7*
14	at Philadelphia	17
21	at Cleveland	27
35	WASHINGTON	21
6	HOUSTON	10
17	at Atlanta	28
23	at Detroit	17 (OT)*
61	GREEN BAY	7*
14	CINCINNATI	17 (OT)
14	at Tampa Bay	13*
304		264

*Intradivisional Games

Tampa Bay Buccaneers (5–10–1)

17	at Cincinnati	12	
10	LOS ANGELES	9	
17	at Dallas	28	
27	CLEVELAND	34	
0	at Chicago	23*	
14	GREEN BAY	14	(OT)*
14	at Houston	20	
24	at San Francisco	23	
30	NEW YORK GIANTS	13	
21	PITTSBURGH	24	
30	at Minnesota	38*	
10	DETROIT	24*	
20	at Green Bay	17*	
10	MINNESOTA	21*	
14	at Detroit	27*	
13	CHICAGO	14*	
271		341	

Green Bay Packers (5–10–1)

12	CHICAGO	6	(OT)*
7	DETROIT	29*	
21	at Los Angeles	51	
7	DALLAS	28	
14	CINCINNATI	9	
14	at Tampa Bay	14	(OT)*
21	at Cleveland	26	
16	MINNESOTA	3*	
20	at Pittsburgh	22	
23	SAN FRANCISCO	16	
21	at New York Giants	27	
25	at Minnesota	13*	
17	TAMPA BAY	20*	
7	at Chicago	61*	
3	HOUSTON	22	
3	at Detroit	24*	
231		371	

*Intradivisional Games

Ring the Bell at Tampa Bay!

Western Division

Atlanta Falcons (12–4)

23	at Minnesota	24
37	at New England	21
17	MIAMI	20
20	at San Francisco	17*
43	DETROIT	28
7	NEW YORK JETS	14
41	at New Orleans	14*
13	LOS ANGELES	10*
30	at Buffalo	14
33	at St. Louis	27 (OT)
31	NEW ORLEANS	13*
28	CHICAGO	17
10	WASHINGTON	6
20	at Philadelphia	17
35	SAN FRANCISCO	10*
17	at Los Angeles	20 (OT)*
405		**272**

Los Angeles Rams (11–5)

20	DETROIT	41
9	at Tampa Bay	10
51	GREEN BAY	21
28	at New York Giants	7
48	SAN FRANCISCO	26*
21	at St. Louis	13
31	at San Francisco	17*
10	at Atlanta	13*
45	NEW ORLEANS	31*
14	MIAMI	35
17	at New England	14
27	at New Orleans	7*
38	NEW YORK JETS	13
7	at Buffalo	10 (OT)
38	DALLAS	14
20	ATLANTA	17 (OT)*
424		**289**

*Intradivisional Games

San Francisco 49ers (6–10)

26	at New Orleans	23*	
24	ST. LOUIS	21	(OT)
37	at New York Jets	27	
17	ATLANTA	20*	
26	at Los Angeles	48*	
14	at Dallas	59	
17	LOS ANGELES	31*	
23	TAMPA BAY	24	
13	at Detroit	17	
16	at Green Bay	23	
13	at Miami	17	
12	NEW YORK GIANTS	0	
21	NEW ENGLAND	17	
38	NEW ORLEANS	35	(OT)*
10	at Atlanta	35*	
13	BUFFALO	18	
320		415	

New Orleans Saints (1–15)

23	SAN FRANCISCO	26*	
3	at Chicago	22	
26	BUFFALO	35	
16	at Miami	21	
7	ST. LOUIS	40	
13	at Detroit	24	
14	ATLANTA	41*	
14	at Washington	22	
31	at Los Angeles	45*	
21	PHILADELPHIA	34	
13	at Atlanta	31*	
7	LOS ANGELES	27*	
20	MINNESOTA	23	
35	at San Francisco	38	(OT)*
21	at New York Jets	20	
27	NEW ENGLAND	38	
291		487	

*Intradivisional Games

CLUB-BY-CLUB 1980 STANDINGS

AFC
Eastern Division

Buffalo Bills (11–5)

17	MIAMI	7*
20	NEW YORK JETS	10*
35	at New Orleans	26
24	OAKLAND	7
26	at San Diego	24
12	BALTIMORE	17*
14	at Miami	17*
31	NEW ENGLAND	13*
14	ATLANTA	30
31	at New York Jets	24*
14	at Cincinnati	0
28	PITTSBURGH	13
24	at Baltimore	28*
10	LOS ANGELES	7 (OT)
2	at New England	24*
18	at San Francisco	13
320		**260**

New England Patriots (10–6)

34	CLEVELAND	17
21	ATLANTA	37
37	at Seattle	31
23	DENVER	14
21	at New York Jets	11*
34	MIAMI	0*
37	at Baltimore	21*
13	at Buffalo	31*
34	NEW YORK JETS	21*
34	at Houston	38
14	LOS ANGELES	17
47	BALTIMORE	21*
17	at San Francisco	21
13	at Miami	16 (OT)*
24	BUFFALO	2*
38	at New Orleans	27
441		**325**

*Intradivisional Games

Miami Dolphins (8–8)

7	at Buffalo	17*	
17	CINCINNATI	16	
20	at Atlanta	17	
21	NEW ORLEANS	16	
17	BALTIMORE	30*	
0	at New England	34*	
17	BUFFALO	14*	
14	at New York Jets	17*	
10	at Oakland	16	
35	at Los Angeles	14	
17	SAN FRANCISCO	13	
24	SAN DIEGO	27	(OT)
10	at Pittsburgh	23	
16	NEW ENGLAND	13	(OT)*
24	at Baltimore	14*	
17	NEW YORK JETS	24*	
266		**305**	

Baltimore Colts (7–9)

17	at New York Jets	14*
17	PITTSBURGH	20
16	at Houston	21
35	NEW YORK JETS	21*
30	at Miami	17*
17	at Buffalo	12*
21	NEW ENGLAND	37*
10	ST. LOUIS	17
31	at Kansas City	24
27	CLEVELAND	28
10	at Detroit	9
21	at New England	47*
28	BUFFALO	24*
33	at Cincinnati	34
14	MIAMI	24*
28	KANSAS CITY	38
355		**387**

*Intradivisional Games

New York Jets (4–12)

14	BALTIMORE	17*
10	at Buffalo	20*
27	SAN FRANCISCO	37
21	at Baltimore	35*
11	NEW ENGLAND	21*
14	at Atlanta	7
17	SEATTLE	27
17	MIAMI	14*
21	at New England	34*
24	BUFFALO	31*
24	at Denver	31
31	HOUSTON	28 (OT)
13	at Los Angeles	38
14	at Cleveland	17
20	NEW ORLEANS	21
24	at Miami	17*
302		395

Central Division

Cleveland Browns (11–5)

17	at New England	34
7	HOUSTON	16*
20	KANSAS CITY	13
34	at Tampa Bay	27
16	DENVER	19
27	at Seattle	3
26	GREEN BAY	21
27	PITTSBURGH	26*
27	CHICAGO	21
28	at Baltimore	27
13	at Pittsburgh	16*
31	CINCINNATI	7*
17	at Houston	14*
17	NEW YORK JETS	14
23	at Minnesota	28
27	at Cincinnati	24*
357		310

*Intradivisional Games

The Great Steeler Star Rocky Bleier in His Last Season

Houston Oilers (11–5)

17	at Pittsburgh	31*
16	at Cleveland	7*
21	BALTIMORE	16
13	at Cincinnati	10*
7	SEATTLE	26
20	at Kansas City	21
20	TAMPA BAY	14
23	CINCINNATI	3*
20	at Denver	16
38	NEW ENGLAND	34
10	at Chicago	6
28	at New York Jets	31 (OT)
14	CLEVELAND	17*
6	PITTSBURGH	0*
22	at Green Bay	3
20	MINNESOTA	16
295		**251**

Pittsburgh Steelers (9–7)

31	HOUSTON	17*
20	at Baltimore	17
28	at Cincinnati	30*
38	CHICAGO	3
23	at Minnesota	17
16	CINCINNATI	17*
34	OAKLAND	45
26	at Cleveland	27*
22	GREEN BAY	20
24	at Tampa Bay	21
16	CLEVELAND	13*
13	at Buffalo	28
23	MIAMI	10
0	at Houston	6*
21	KANSAS CITY	16
17	at San Diego	26
352		**313**

*Intradivisional Games

Cincinnati Bengals (6–10)

12	TAMPA BAY	17
16	at Miami	17
30	PITTSBURGH	28*
10	HOUSTON	13*
9	at Green Bay	14
17	at Pittsburgh	16*
14	MINNESOTA	0
3	at Houston	23*
14	SAN DIEGO	31
17	at Oakland	28
0	BUFFALO	14
7	at Cleveland	31*
20	at Kansas City	6
34	BALTIMORE	33
17	at Chicago	14 (OT)
24	CLEVELAND	27*
244		312

Western Division

San Diego Chargers (11–5)

34	at Seattle	13*
30	OAKLAND	24 (OT)*
30	at Denver	13*
24	at Kansas City	7*
24	BUFFALO	26
24	at Oakland	38*
44	NEW YORK GIANTS	7
31	at Dallas	42
31	at Cincinnati	14
13	DENVER	20*
20	KANSAS CITY	7*
27	at Miami	24
22	PHILADELPHIA	21
17	at Washington	40
21	SEATTLE	14*
26	PITTSBURGH	17
418		327

*Intradivisional Games

Oakland Raiders (11–5)

27	at Kansas City	14*
24	at San Diego	30 (OT)*
24	WASHINGTON	21
7	at Buffalo	24
17	KANSAS CITY	31*
38	SAN DIEGO	24*
45	at Pittsburgh	34
33	SEATTLE	14*
16	MIAMI	10
28	CINCINNATI	17
19	at Seattle	17*
7	at Philadelphia	10
9	DENVER	3*
13	DALLAS	19
24	at Denver	21*
33	at New York Giants	17
364		306

Kansas City Chiefs (8–8)

14	OAKLAND	27*
16	SEATTLE	17*
13	at Cleveland	20
7	SAN DIEGO	24*
31	at Oakland	17
21	HOUSTON	20
23	at Denver	17*
20	DETROIT	17
24	BALTIMORE	31
31	at Seattle	30*
7	at San Diego	20*
21	at St. Louis	13
6	CINCINNATI	20*
31	DENVER	14*
16	at Pittsburgh	21
38	at Baltimore	28
319		336

*Intradivisional Games

Denver Broncos (8–8)

6	at Philadelphia	27
41	DALLAS	20
13	SAN DIEGO	30*
14	at New England	23
19	at Cleveland	16
20	WASHINGTON	17
17	KANSAS CITY	23*
14	at New York Giants	9
16	HOUSTON	20
20	at San Diego	13*
31	NEW YORK JETS	24
36	SEATTLE	20*
3	at Oakland	9*
14	at Kansas City	31*
21	OAKLAND	24*
25	at Seattle	17*
310		323

Seattle Seahawks (4–12)

13	SAN DIEGO	34*
17	at Kansas City	16*
31	NEW ENGLAND	37
14	at Washington	0
26	at Houston	7
3	CLEVELAND	27
27	at New York Jets	17
14	at Oakland	33*
20	PHILADELPHIA	27
30	KANSAS CITY	31*
17	OAKLAND	19*
20	at Denver	36*
7	at Dallas	51
21	NEW YORK GIANTS	27
14	at San Diego	21*
17	DENVER	25*
291		408

*Intradivisional Games